Excel

Get the Results You Want!

JUNIOR HIGH SCHOOL GRAMMAR HANDBOOK

ridden
The boy has ~~rode~~ that horse before.

sung
Miriam and I have ~~sang~~ the song.

blown
The winds have ~~blew~~ for many hours.

PASCAL PRESS

Phil Walker

Reprinted 2008, 2010, 2011, 2012, 2017, 2019, 2023, 2024

ISBN 978 1 74125 259 0

Pascal Press
PO Box 250
Glebe NSW 2037
(02) 9198 1748
www.pascalpress.com.au

Publisher: Vivienne Joannou
Project editor: Mark Dixon
Edited by Christine Eslick
Answers checked by Dorothy Jones
Typeset by Ij Design (Julianne Billington)
Cover by DiZign Pty Ltd
Printed by Vivar Printing/Green Giant Press

Contents

Contents

Contents

Introduction

The ***Excel* Junior High School Grammar Handbook** has been designed to help students achieve a high level of mastery over basic grammatical concepts and terminology. It has been prepared so that a single page covers one specific aspect of grammar.

The layout and structure will prove valuable to the following groups of students:

- **students** requiring a comprehensive coverage of grammar
- **students studying languages other than English** who will find a sound knowledge of English grammar is a significant advantage
- **students from non-English speaking backgrounds** who will benefit from the structured page-by-page approach to the complexities of English
- **students in the final years of secondary school** who require a systematic presentation of English grammar
- **mature age students** requiring a refresher course in grammatical structure.

Terms and activities are introduced in a logical sequence. It is not necessary to turn to later pages to understand the content. There is also a grammar dictionary providing succinct and easily understood definitions of all terms used in this book.

Each chapter contains the following tests:

Quick check	These are short tests at the bottom of some pages.
How much do you know?	These are one-page tests at the end of a subsection.
Section test	These are tests of one or two pages at the end of each section.
Review test	These are two-page tests covering the work of a complete chapter.

Answers and explanations (where necessary) have been included for self-assessment.

1 Parts of speech

Nouns – Common and proper

A **noun** is a **naming word**. It is the name of a **person**, **animal**, **place**, **thing**, **feeling** or **idea**.

Common nouns

Common nouns are the **names** of **everyday things**.

Examples

- The **girls** and **boys** played in the **park**.
- His **sister** flew a **kite** in the **backyard**.

1 **Underline** the **common nouns** in these sentences.

a The new watch was on the table by the telephone.

b Take the parcel to the shop down the road.

2 **Select common nouns** from the box below to fit these sentences.

a The ________________ was lying beside the ________________.

b That ________________ took her ________________ to the ________________.

c My ________________ bought the ________________ at the local ________________.

girl	father	meat	desk
book	towel	supermarket	beach

Proper nouns

Proper nouns are the **names** of **particular persons** or **places** and **begin** with a **capital letter**.

Examples

- **Sandy** visited the museum on **Tuesday**.
- Last **August Mike** travelled to the **Blue Mountains**.

3 **Select proper nouns** from the box below to fit these sentences.

a ________________ and ________________ were at the show.

b ________________, our pet cat, was given to us by ________________.

Jill	Sydney	Jan	Mittens	Tim	Monday

Quick check

Underline the **common nouns**. **Circle** the **proper nouns**.

It was Wednesday and the huge golden sun was shining. The children were looking across to the township of Lonton. There were lots of people on the jetty. Raynor and Sharnie were pointing at the shape of a shark moving through the water towards the jetty. Mike and John rushed out to see the huge creature.

Answers on page 112

Nouns – Collective and abstract

A noun is a **naming word**. It is the name of a **person**, **animal**, **place**, **thing**, **feeling** or **idea**.

Collective nouns

Collective nouns are the **names** of a **collection** of **people** or **things**.

Examples

- A **pack** of wolves roamed the highlands.
- The **troop** of monkeys was frightened by the approach of the **pride** of lions.

team	bunch	mob	bouquet	company
herd	group	troupe	collection	school
fleet	bundle	swarm	platoon	flock

1 **Underline** the **collective nouns**.

a She saw a flock of sheep and a herd of cattle.
b Becky bought a hand of bananas and a bunch of grapes.
c The litter of puppies walked across the colony of ants.

2 **Add** a **collective noun** to these sentences.

a A ________________ of birds flew over the school.
b The ________________ of bees gathered at the nest.
c Did the ________________ of netballers catch the bus?

Abstract nouns

Abstract nouns are the **names** of **things you cannot see**, **taste**, **hear**, **smell** or **touch**.

Examples

- The young girl was praised for her **honesty**.
- She took great **pride** in her work.
- All the people were filled with **happiness**.

3 **Underline** the **abstract nouns**.

a Laura received a medal for her bravery.
b All the townspeople were filled with sorrow.
c The beauty of the sunset delighted the visitors.

4 **Select** suitable **abstract nouns** from the box below to **complete** the sentences.

a He said it was a ________________ to play on the swing.
b It was a great ________________ for them to rest after the long march.
c The death of the child caused great ________________ in the town

sorrow	enjoyment	pride	satisfaction
happiness	relief	sadness	pleasure

☞ Answers on page 112

Nouns – Verbal nouns

More nouns. Once again, **nouns** are the **names** of **something**.

Verbal nouns are the **names** of **activities** and consist of a **verb plus** the **ending *-ing*** (e.g. *collect* (verb) + ***-ing*** = *collect**ing***).

Examples

- **Collecting** butterflies is an interesting pastime.
- She enjoys **riding** trail bikes.
- **Running** is a great form of exercise.

1 **Underline** the **verbal nouns**.

a Growing grapes is quite difficult.

b She enjoyed dancing on the stage.

c They were fond of building model cars.

2 **Select** suitable **verbal nouns** from the box below to **complete** these sentences.

a They heard a high-pitched ________________.

b ________________ the tall mountain was not easy.

c Skye found that ____________________ the items took many hours.

seeing	adjusting	climbing	screaming	flapping

Some ***ing* words** can be a **verbal noun** or **part** of a **compound verb**. (A compound verb is made up of two or more words.)

Examples

- **Buying** the car was quite exciting. (verbal noun)
- She **is buying** a new pair of shoes. (part of compound verb)

3 **Identify** the ***-ing* words** as **verbal nouns** or **part** of a **compound verb**.

a Purchasing the new house took some time. ________________

b Jan and John are purchasing a new home. ________________

c Toko was celebrating his birthday. ________________

d They all enjoyed celebrating the discovery. ________________

e The lifesavers were preventing swimmers from drowning. ____________ ____________

Quick check

1 **Underline** the **verbal nouns**.

a Raising the wreck was a difficult task.

b After completing the work they left for home.

c Accelerating quickly down the slope was great fun.

d By dividing the load equally they could gather the provisions.

2 **Write** a **sentence** using the word *collecting* as a **verbal noun**. ______________________________

____

Answers on page 112

Nouns – Noun groups

A **noun group** is a **group** of **words** with a **noun** as the **main word**. Other words, such as describing words, phrases and clauses, may be included in the noun group.

Examples

- **Attractive vases** were on display in the store.
- **The young athletic boy** lives in our street.

*The words in **bold** are **noun groups** with **describing words**.*

1 **Use describing words** to **form** a **noun group** in these sentences.

a The ________________ vehicle was in the garage.

b Several buses travelled along the ________________ road.

Examples

- **Several ships** sailed into the harbour.
- **The ninth car** in the row was a Ford.

*The words in **bold** are **noun groups** with **describing words telling** us **how many**.*

2 **Add describing words** of **quantity** to **form noun groups**.

a ________________ people walked into the building.

b ________________ huts were being built near the pool.

Examples

- **The girls in the red skirts** played netball.
- **The boat that I have** is brand new.

*The words in **bold** are **noun groups** with **phrases** or **clauses** included.*

3 **Select** suitable **phrases** or **clauses** from the box below to **form noun groups**.

a This garment ________________________ is too small.

b Several houses ________________________________ were built in our street.

c I have often seen the shop ________________________.

of the district	which came to town	to the end
with red buttons	that were of modern design	that has a pink door

Quick check

1 **Underline** the **noun groups** in these sentences.

a A large number of beautiful paintings was on display.

b Have you seen the car with the red roof?

c Many of the goods that were on the shelf remained unsold.

d Some of the people from out of town attended the concert.

2 **Use** this **noun group** in a suitable sentence: *these delightful fresh flowers*. ________________

____

Answers on page 112

Nouns

1 **Underline** the **common nouns** in these sentences. Checkpoint page 1

- **a** The tribe lived in the clearing in the jungle.
- **b** Some of the cars were in the garages.
- **c** Have the pictures on the wall been cleaned?

2 **Circle** the **proper nouns** in this paragraph. Checkpoint page 1

Jim and Jae travelled to Atherton last Thursday. They bought a new Ford sedan and drove back to Lake Barrine. Here they showed the new vehicle to Leeanne and John. The two then returned home along Eachem Road.

3 **Underline** the **collective nouns** in these sentences. Checkpoint page 2

- **a** A flight of birds flew over the herd of buffalo.
- **b** The litter of kittens was hidden near the bunches of flowers.
- **c** Several groups of players boarded the fleet of small boats.

4 **Circle** the **abstract nouns** in this paragraph. Checkpoint page 2

The family was filled with grief at the death of their elderly relative. Grief turned to anger when they realised it was a careless accident. They showed great kindness and love to each other at this sad time.

5 **Circle** the **verbal nouns** in these sentences. Checkpoint page 3

- **a** The children enjoyed camping and fishing.
- **b** Collecting and mounting butterflies was his hobby.
- **c** Caring for the injured animal was a difficult task.

6 **Add** suitable **verbal nouns** to these sentences. Checkpoint page 3

- **a** ____________________ the papers took some time.
- **b** ____________________ the soil into equal quantities was left to the workers.
- **c** ____________________ fine roses was her favourite hobby.

7 **Select** a **suitable noun** from the box to complete each sentence. The type of noun is indicated in brackets. Checkpoint pages 1–4

swimming	horror	cars	admiration	adults	Lisa
swapping	batch	trucks	children	pride	Sharon

- **a** ____________________ and ____________________ visited the show. (common)
- **b** ____________________ and ____________________ swam in the lake. (proper)
- **c** ____________________ in the creek was great fun. (verbal noun)
- **d** A ____________________ of lions lay under the tree. (collective)
- **e** She was filled with ____________________ when she saw the beautiful young foal. (abstract)

Answers on page 112

Pronouns – Personal, possessive, reflexive

A **pronoun** is a word that can be **used instead** of a **noun**.

Personal pronouns

I	you	she	it	us	her
we	he	they	me	him	them

1 **Underline** the **personal pronouns** in these sentences.

a He is going to leave the school.
b Did you see them at the museum?
c We will give it to Jane's brother.

Examples
- **You** are going with **him** tomorrow.
- **She** had given **it** to **me**.

2 **Add** suitable **personal pronouns** to these sentences.

a ________________ and ________________ will leave at three o'clock.
b ________________ will collect all the pencils.
c ________________ all played in the park.

Possessive pronouns

Possessive pronouns show **ownership**.

his	hers	mine	ours	yours	theirs
her	my	our	your	their	its

3 **Circle** the **possessive pronouns** in these sentences.

a Did Jack say that the car is yours?
b Our parents collected the prizes.
c Is your sister attending the class?

Examples
- That book is **mine**.
- All of the cards are **theirs**.

4 **Add** suitable **possessive pronouns** to these sentences.

a ________________ cousin lived in Granville. **b** This is ________________ new book.
c ________________ parents took us to the beach.

Reflexive pronouns

Reflexive pronouns refer to the **previous noun** or **pronoun**.

end in *self* or *selves*

5 **Underline** the **reflexive pronouns** in these sentences.

a She hurt herself with the machine.
b Travel to the beach by yourselves.
c All the children played by themselves.

Examples
- She travelled by **herself** to town.
- They will enjoy **themselves** at the show.

6 **Add** suitable **reflexive pronouns** to these sentences.

a You can go by ________________________ to his place.
b The animal had injured ________________________.

Answers on page 112

Pronouns – Relative and interrogative

A **pronoun** is a word **used instead** of a **noun**.

Relative pronouns

A **relative pronoun begins** an **adjectival clause** in a sentence with two or more clauses. (An adjectival clause tells us about a noun in the other clause.)

Look at this sentence: This is the car, **which** I bought.

which is a **relative pronoun** beginning the clause *which I bought*. It **tells us about** *car*.

who	whom	whose	which	that

Examples

The **adjectival clause** describes a **noun** in the **first clause**:

- These are the books (first clause) — **that** I have collected. (adjectival clause) — that ➡ books
- These are the boys (first clause) — **who** played on the swing. (adjectival clause) — who ➡ boys

1 **Circle** the **relative pronouns** and **underline** the **adjectival clauses**.

a Here is the kitten that I own.

b Do you know the girl who owns the helmet?

c Where is the boy whose father is away?

2 **Add** suitable **relative pronouns** to these sentences.

Hint: If the relative pronoun refers to a **person**, use the words *who*, *whom* or *whose*.

a Last week we saw the girl __________________ mother was ill.

b Here is the animal __________________ escaped from the pen.

c She fell on to the tiles __________________ had only just been laid.

3 **Add** suitable **adjectival clauses** beginning with the **relative pronouns** in **bold**.

a These are the trucks **that** ____

b The workers arranged the display **which** ____

c I saw the young girl **who** ____

Interrogative pronouns

An **interrogative pronoun** is used to **ask** a **question**. It is almost always used at the **beginning** of a **sentence**.

Examples

- **Who** is going to the fair?
- **What** is the exact time?
- Could you tell me **who** is going?

4 **Underline** the **interrogative pronouns** in these sentences.

a Which of these cars belongs to Nick?

b Who will light the fire?

c What will happen to the injured bird?

☞ Answers on page 112

Pronouns – Demonstrative, distributive, indefinite

A **pronoun** is a word that can be **used instead** of a **noun**.

Demonstrative pronouns

A **demonstrative pronoun** stands **in place** of the **name** of an **object**.

this	that	these	those

Examples

- **This** is the most attractive car.
- **These** are very attractive flowers.

1 **Circle** the **demonstrative pronouns** in these sentences.

a Those are the least likely to grow well.

b Are these the best available?

c That is a wonderful present.

2 **Add** suitable **demonstrative pronouns** to these sentences.

a ________________ are the prettiest flowers.

b ________________ can be used in any situation.

c ________________ will be a very successful invention.

Distributive pronouns

A **distributive pronoun** is used to **point out** a **particular item**.

each	either	neither

Examples

- **Each** of the plants was removed.
- **Either** of the cars will be sold today.

3 **Underline** the **distributive pronouns** in these sentences.

a Neither of the boys was injured in the crash.

b Has each of the items been washed?

c She said that either of the discs could be used.

Indefinite pronouns

An **indefinite pronoun** is one that **does not stand for** a **particular person**, **thing** or **place**.

end in *one*, *body* or *thing*

Examples

- **Nobody** was walking along the road.
- He found that **someone** had broken the window.
- **Anyone** can finish it if effort is applied.

4 **Circle** the **indefinite pronouns** in these sentences.

a Has anybody seen his new brush?

b Everything was completed for the concert.

c I saw no-one at the creek yesterday.

d I thought something was wrong.

☞ Answers on page 112

Pronouns

1 **Underline** the **personal pronouns, circle** the **possessive pronouns** and **shade** the **reflexive pronouns** in these sentences.

Checkpoint page 6

a They went by themselves to the swimming pool.

b The clothes I saw were not ours.

c You will be able to go by yourself tomorrow.

2 **Insert** suitable **personal**, **possessive** and **reflexive pronouns** in these sentences.

Checkpoint page 6

a ____________ will collect all the books ____________.

b ____________ took all the books that were ____________.

c ____________ admired the work done by ____________ sister.

3 **Circle** the **relative pronouns** and **underline** the **adjectival clauses**.

Checkpoint page 7

a There is the boat that I own.

b Has she seen the painting which has been cleaned?

c Can you see the girl whose mother is at the gate?

4 **Add** suitable **relative pronouns** to these sentences.

Checkpoint page 7

a In the morning we will see the car ____________ is new.

b Where is the boy ____________ dog has been lost?

c The girl ____________ won the race is very determined.

5 **Circle** the **interrogative pronouns** in these sentences.

Checkpoint page 7

a Who will be going to the show later?

b What can be done to complete the task?

c Which of the shirts belongs to Alan?

6 **Underline** the **demonstrative pronouns** in these sentences.

Checkpoint page 8

a These are the most elegant gowns.

b That is a particularly interesting novel.

c Those are the prettiest flowers in the garden.

7 **Use** suitable **distributive pronouns** in these sentences.

Checkpoint page 8

a ____________ of the cars will be repaired shortly.

b He said that ____________ of the trees was damaged.

c ____________ of the girls will compete in the contest.

8 **Circle** the **indefinite pronouns** in these sentences.

Checkpoint page 8

a Has anybody collected the mail yet?

b Someone has found the boy by the gate.

c Somebody has fallen into the crevasse.

☞ Answers on page 113

Adjectives – Numbering, descriptive, proper

An **adjective** is a **describing word**. It tells us **what kind of**, **how many**, **how much** or **which** person or object is being described.

Numbering adjectives

1 **Underline** the **numbering adjectives** in these sentences.

- **a** Does Joe have fifteen felt pens?
- **b** Maddie bought nine new magazines.
- **c** Steve came third in the cross country race.

Examples

- There are **seven** cards in the box.
- Have you got **thirty** dollars?
- Here is the **fourth** toy in the set.

2 **Add** suitable **numbering adjectives** to these sentences.

- **a** Does the girl have ________________ new ribbons?
- **b** My cousin Andy collected ________________ CDs.
- **c** His brother came ________________ in the long jump event.

Descriptive adjectives

3 **Underline** the **descriptive adjectives** in these sentences.

- **a** The bright sun shone down on a peaceful scene.
- **b** The motor vessel came into the safe harbour.
- **c** His young brother collected the beautiful shells.

Examples

- There is the **new** cruiser.
- Did you find the **correct** answer?
- It was a **dull** concert.

4 **Add** suitable **descriptive adjectives** to these sentences.

- **a** On the ____________ oval they played ________________________ games.
- **b** The ____________ room was left in a ________________________ mess.
- **c** All the ____________ books were on the ________________________ table.

Proper adjectives

5 **Underline** the **proper adjectives** in these sentences.

- **a** The Spanish stallion was a fine animal.
- **b** Here are the Irish exchange students.
- **c** The South Australian event was very interesting.

Examples

- The **English** coin was on the table.
- It is the **Australian** flag.
- The **Japanese** car sold very well.

Quick check

Underline the **numbering adjectives**. **Circle** the **descriptive adjectives**. **Shade** the **proper adjectives**.

The first motor launch reached the calm harbour. There were eleven more to follow. Soon the beautiful harbour was a delightful picture as the local and African launches cruised in to tie up at the crowded wharf.

Answers on page 113

Adjectives – Demonstrative, distributive, indefinite

An **adjective** is a **describing word**. It tells **what kind of**, **how many**, **how much** or **which** person or object is being described.

Demonstrative adjectives

These **point out** or **identify**.

Examples
- **This** horse has been running well.
- **Those** pencils have been broken.
- Did you follow **these** clues?

1. **Underline** the **demonstrative adjectives** in these sentences.
   - **a** Did you see those plants yesterday?
   - **b** Is this car the one that Julie bought?
   - **c** I saw this book on the table.

Distributive adjectives

These **point out** or identify **separate things**.

Examples
- I saw **every** book on the shelf.
- **Either** Tanya or Julie will leave.
- **Each** animal was led across the ring.

2. **Underline** the **distributive adjectives** in these sentences.
   - **a** Neither Jason nor Justin arrived at the party.
   - **b** Did you see either Fran or Diane?
   - **c** He found every object in the tray.

3. **Add** suitable **demonstrative** or **distributive adjectives** to these sentences.
   - **a** He took ____________________ book and read ____________________ one.
   - **b** ____________________ child will receive a present.

Indefinite adjectives

These show **no actual number**.

Examples
- There were **several** aircraft there.
- **Many** people attended the show.
- **Some** cake was left on the table.

4. **Circle** the **indefinite adjectives** in these sentences.
   - **a** He saw few people beside the river.
   - **b** Most passengers waited at the gate.
   - **c** There was less soil in the top paddock.

5. **Add** suitable **indefinite adjectives** to these sentences.
   - **a** There were ______________ people at the show.
   - **b** ______________ of the cakes were chocolate.

Quick check

Add suitable **demonstrative, distributive** and **indefinite adjectives**.

______________ animals were placed in ______________ race but ______________ others did not cover the distance. ______________ horse was taken away on a float.

Answers on page 113

Adjectives – Interrogative

An **adjective** is a **describing word**. It tells **what kind of**, **how many**, **how much** or **which** person or object is being described.

Interrogative adjectives

Interrogative adjectives are used when **asking questions**.

Examples

- **What** type of animal is that?
- **Which** car came in the gate?
- **Whose** father is waiting at the pool?

1 **Underline** the **interrogative adjectives** in these sentences.

a Which car has been left at the shop?

b What type of motorhome is that?

c Whose brother has collected the mail?

Hint: Note the difference between **interrogative adjectives** and **interrogative pronouns**.

Interrogative adjective:	Which vehicle belongs to Sue? (adjective + noun)	(noun follows adjective)
Interrogative pronoun:	Which is the correct vehicle? (pronoun)	(no noun after the pronoun)

2 **Label** the words in **bold** as **adjectives** or **pronouns**.

a **Whose** cousin attended the school? ______________________

b **Whose** is this new coat? ______________________

c **What** answer did you get? ______________________

d **What** was said by the girl. ______________________

Articles

Articles are similar to adjectives. There are three articles: ***a***, ***an*** and ***the***.

a and ***an*** are called **indefinite articles** because they **do not refer to** a **particular object**.

the is called the **definite article** because it **refers to** a **specific object**.

Examples

- **A** pile of washing was on **the** floor.
- Did you see **an** apple on **the** table.
- She had never seen **the** collection.
- She bought **a** CD at **the** music store.
- **The** new car is in **the** yard.

Quick check

Underline the **interrogative adjectives**. **Circle** the **interrogative pronouns**. **Shade** the **articles**.

1 Which of the pencils belongs to that girl?

2 Who completed a clay model yesterday?

3 What item of clothing was on the floor?

4 Whose books were on a ledge in the building?

Answers on page 113

Adjectives – Describing and comparing

Adjectives can be used in sentences **to describe** or **compare persons** or **objects**.

Adjectives can **describe**, e.g. *It is a **hot** day*.

When an adjective is used simply to describe one person or thing, we say that this is the **positive degree** of the adjective.

Adjectives can **compare two things**, e.g. *It is **hotter** today than yesterday*.

When an adjective is used to compare two persons or things we say that we are using the **comparative degree** of the adjective.

Adjectives can **compare more than two things**, e.g. *It is the **hottest** day of the week*.

When an adjective is used to compare more than two persons or things, we are using the **superlative degree** of the adjective.

1 **Complete** the table.

	Positive (describing one)	**Comparative** (comparing two)	**Superlative** (comparing more than two)
a	small		
b	kind		
c	heavy		
d	bright		

Using *more* and *most*

If the adjective sounds clumsy or awkward when ***er*** and ***est*** are added we add the words **more** or **less** for the comparative degree and **most** or **least** for the superlative degree.

Example

- attractive ➡ **more** or **less** attractive ➡ **most** or **least** attractive

2 **Complete** this table.

	Positive	**Comparative**	**Superlative**
a	splendid		
b	careful		
c	fierce		

Unusual forms

Some adjectives **cannot be compared**, e.g. *full*, *empty*, *correct*, *dead*.

Some adjectives **change form completely**.

Positive	**Comparative**	**Superlative**
bad	worse	worst
good	better	best
many	more	most
much	more	most

Answers on page 113

Adjectives

How much do you know?

1 **Add numbering** and **descriptive adjectives** to these sentences. Checkpoint page 10

a The ________________ ________________ athlete won the ________________ race across the ________________ oval.

b Many ________________ boats sailed slowly past the ________________ vessels moored near the lighthouse.

c Could you identify the ________________ piece of ________________ art work in the ________________ collection.

2 **Circle** the **proper adjectives** in these sentences. Checkpoint page 10

a The African coastline came into view.

b Has the Indonesian general inspected the troops?

c All the Chinese entertainers were in the square.

3 **Add demonstrative** or **distributive adjectives** to these sentences. Checkpoint page 11

a Did you see ________________ people from the valley?

b I know ________________ mats have been damaged.

c ________________ kitten had white paws.

d ________________ book is a favourite with many children.

e ________________ Annette or Lee will collect the parcel.

4 **Circle** the **indefinite adjectives** in these sentences. Checkpoint page 11

a Here is some cake for you.

b I have caught many butterflies.

c We have more marbles than Jack has.

5 **Label** the words in **bold** as **interrogative adjectives** or **interrogative pronouns**. Checkpoint page 12

a **What** colour do you want?________________

b **What** is the time?________________

c **Which** glue stick is yours?________________

d **Which** will be available?________________

6 **Add articles** to the following. Checkpoint page 12

a __________ small boy found his way to __________ farm.

b __________ elephant was in __________ paddock.

c __________ pear and __________ apple were on __________ plate.

7 **Complete** the **table** of adjectives. Checkpoint page 13

	Positive	Comparative	Superlative
a	large		
b	tall		
c		more or less useful	
d			worst
e		more	

☞ Answers on page 113

Verbs – Main, auxiliary, compound

A **verb** tells us **what is being done**. It is a **doing**, **having** or **being** word.

Verbs can be **action verbs**, **feeling** or **thinking verbs**, **stating** or **telling verbs**, or **relating verbs**.

Examples

- The girl **drove** the go-cart. (action verb)
- She **remembered** to return the book. (thinking or feeling verb)
- They **yelled** across the road. (stating or telling verb)
- He **is** a good painter. (relating verb)

1 **Underline** the **verb** and **state** its **type**.

- **a** The carrier delivered the parcel. ______________________
- **b** He howled when hurt by the log. ______________________
- **c** Mary forgot to organise the letters. ______________________
- **d** Lily became a fine doctor. ______________________

2 **Add verbs** of the **type indicated**.

- **a** She will ______________ all the names in the list. (thinking or feeling)
- **b** My cousin ______________ the heavy weight. (action)
- **c** Amber ______________ to the climber at the top. (stating or telling)
- **d** His sister ______________ a successful dancer. (relating)

Auxiliary verbs

Main verbs stand alone but some verbs are made up of **two** or **more verbs**. The **extra verbs** added to the main verb are called **auxiliary verbs**.

Examples

- The girl **danced** on the stage. (danced = **main verb**)
- The girl **had danced** on the stage. (had = **auxiliary verb**, danced = **main verb**)

3 **Circle** the **main verbs** in these sentences. **Underline** the **auxiliary verb**.

- **a** Sven and his brother will travel to Europe.
- **b** All of the people can complete the task easily.
- **c** The cleaner did remove the rubbish early.

4 **Add** suitable **main** and **auxiliary verbs**.

- **a** The boy ____________________________ the work he was given.
- **b** My cousin ____________________________ the book to her home.
- **c** Their new neighbours ____________________________ the furniture.

Compound verbs

Where there is a **main verb** and **one** or **more auxiliary verbs**, the complete verb is called a **compound verb**.

5 **Circle** the **compound verbs** in these sentences.

- **a** She will have broken the toy before long.
- **b** The bottles have been collected for processing.
- **c** His sister may have sprinted for at least one minute.

Answers on page 113

Verbs – Tense

Verbs are written in such a way that you can tell **when an action** or **happening is taking place**. This is what is called the **tense of the verb**.

There are three main tenses: **present tense**, **past tense** and **future tense**.

Examples

- The horse **leaves** the stable. (present tense = **now**)
- The horse **left** the stable. (past tense = **in the past**)
- The horse **will leave** the stable. (future tense = **in the future**)

1 **Underline** the **verbs** in the sentences. **Mark** the **verb** as **present, past** or **future**.

- **a** Some of the children enjoy the game. ____________________
- **b** My father collected the new car. ____________________
- **c** Marta will build the new computer. ____________________
- **d** The vehicle was driven along the track. ____________________
- **e** Nick had completed the work early. ____________________

2 **Add** suitable **verbs** of the **tense indicated** to these sentences.

- **a** All the townspeople ________________________ the meeting. (present)
- **b** The old farmer ________________________ all his crops. (past)
- **c** The young skaters ________________________ their skates here. (future)
- **d** They ________________________ the tracks along the river. (past)

3 **Complete** the sets of three sentences **using** the **tense** indicated.

- **a** Many of the children **travel** to the fair. (present)
- **b** ____ (past)
- **c** ____ (future)
- **d** The mechanic **fixes** the problem. (present)
- **e** ____ (past)
- **f** ____ (future)

4 **Change** the **tense** of the **verb** in these sentences to the **tense indicated**.

- **a** The car speeds along the race track. The car ____________________ along the race track. (future)
- **b** All the children collected the papers. All the children ____________________ the papers. (present)
- **c** My aunt will fertilise the new plants. My aunt ____________________ the new plants. (past)

Quick check

Underline the **verbs** and **identify** the **tense**.

1. Sally will read the new novel. ____________________
2. His younger sister had taken the medicine. ____________________
3. The diamond will be polished shortly. ____________________
4. All the plants were watered by the sprinklers. ____________________

Answers on pages 113–114

Verbs – Participles, regular and irregular verbs

Verbs are often **made up** of **auxiliary verbs** and **participles**.

Participles

Past participles indicate **past tense** and **present participles** indicate **present tense**.

Examples

- The girl has (auxiliary verb) collected (past participle) the money.
- The girl was (auxiliary verb) dancing (present participle) for many years.

1 **Underline** the **participles**. **Mark** them as **past or present participles**.

a All of the boys had painted the building. ______________________

b They were flying until late in the day. ______________________

c She has cried about her loss many times. ______________________

d The children are jumping by the creek. ______________________

2 **Add** suitable **participles** and indicate **past or present**.

a The young boy had ____________________ the lost pen. ______________

b The horse had ____________________ him to the ground. ______________

c She is ____________________ late into the night. ______________

d The glass was ____________________ out by the blast. ______________

Regular and irregular verbs

In **regular verbs**, the past participle ends in ***ed***, ***d*** or ***t***.

Present tense	Past tense	Past participle	Present participle
work	worked	worked	working
collect	collected	collected	collecting
clean	cleaned	cleaned	cleaning
roar	roared	roared	roaring

In **irregular verbs**, the past tense and the past participle are formed in a different way.

Present tense	Past tense	Past participle	Present participle
begin	began	begun	beginning
ring	rang	rung	ringing
throw	threw	thrown	throwing
fly	flew	flown	flying

3 **Write** the **past tense** and the **past participle** of these present tense verbs.

a rub: ______________ ______________ b stop: ______________ ______________

c delay: ______________ ______________ d cry: ______________ ______________

4 **Write** the **past tense** and the **past participle** of these present tense verbs.

a spring: ______________ ______________ b choose: ______________ ______________

c ride: ______________ ______________ d tear: ______________ ______________

Answers on page 114

Verbs – Infinitive (infinite verb) and voice

A verb tells us what is **being done**. It is a **doing**, **having** or **being** word.

Infinitive (infinite verb)

An **infinite verb**, called the **infinitive**, is never the main verb in a sentence. It often begins with the word ***to*** and frequently **begins** a **group** of **words** called a **phrase**.

Examples

- They came to the area **to surf**.
- **To polish** the car took some time.

1 **Underline** the **infinitives** in the following. **Indicate** if the infinitive **begins** a **phrase**.

a	They were there to finish the work.	Yes ☐	No ☐	(tick)
b	To sleep all day was his goal.	Yes ☐	No ☐	
c	She hurried to catch the train.	Yes ☐	No ☐	
d	To succeed was her greatest joy.	Yes ☐	No ☐	

2 **Add** suitable **infinitives** or **phrases beginning** with **infinitives**.

a All of the boys stayed on ________________________________.

b ________________________________ was a difficult task.

c Did you try ________________________________?

d They climbed the mountain ________________________________.

Voice

Verbs may be **active voice** or **passive voice**. The two different voices allow the same thoughts or ideas to be expressed in different ways.

Examples

- **Sian** (the person who performed the action) <u>cleaned</u> **the room**. (the thing acted upon) (**active** voice)
- **The room** (the thing acted upon) <u>was cleaned</u> **by Sian**. (the person who performed the action) (**passive** voice)

3 **Underline** the **verb**. **Indicate** whether the verb is **active** or **passive**.

a The young lion was groomed by the handler. ________________

b My young sister completed the work. ________________

c All the biscuits were eaten by the visitors. ________________

d Those animals trampled the crops. ________________

Quick check

Circle the **infinitives** in these sentences. **Underline** the verbs that are **active voice**.

1 They came to play on the new equipment.

2 They began to enjoy themselves at once.

3 The smaller children were helped by their older sisters.

4 My uncle visited the store to purchase the item.

5 Madeline posted the notices to draw attention to the show.

Answers on page 114

Verbs

1 **Underline** the **verb**. **Identify** the **type** of **verb** (action, thinking or feeling, stating or telling, or relating). Checkpoint page 15

a The young chef cooked a delightful meal. ______________________

b Many of them forgot the way to the sheds. ______________________

c All the fans cried in despair. ______________________

d His older brothers were all pilots. ______________________

2 **Circle** the **main verbs** and **underline** the **auxiliary verbs**. Checkpoint page 15

a She has painted the scene very well.

b Susan will replace the broken glass.

c My father had travelled the road many times.

3 **Underline** the **verbs** in these sentences. Mark the verb as **present**, **past** or **future**. Checkpoint page 16

a Many of the girls followed the instructions. ______________________

b The ship will sail on the morning tide. ______________________

c Elle has decided not to attend. ______________________

d The curators decorate the display. ______________________

4 **Change** these sentences so that the **tense** of the **verb** is **future**. Checkpoint page 16

a The car has been driven along the path. ______________________

b The old sailor plays the violin well. ______________________

5 **Underline** the **past** and **present participles**. Checkpoint page 17

a They had shown him the way to town.

b My cousin was practising yesterday.

c Ayesha had cleaned out the tank early.

6 **Complete** the table. Checkpoint page 17

	Present tense	Past tense	Past participle	Present participle
a	crack			
b	blow			
c	shrink			

7 **Circle** the **infinite verbs** in these sentences. Checkpoint page 18

a Here is a magazine to read.

b The traders came ashore to exchange goods.

c To follow the path is quite difficult.

d Alan ran to catch the early bus.

8 **Underline** the verbs in the **active voice**. **Circle** those in the **passive voice**. Checkpoint page 18

a The house was painted well by Amy.

b The old dog chewed on the bone.

c This yellow can was damaged by the visitors.

d All of the flowers were picked by the old lady.

Answers on page 114

Section test 1A

Nouns, pronouns, adjectives, verbs

1 **Underline** the **common nouns** and **circle** the **proper nouns**.

Some of the children went to Welling Crossing for a picnic. Alan and Rae were in charge of the group. It was a sunny afternoon and the swimming area was quite crowded. The time passed quickly and soon it was time to leave. The group travelled back through Daville to the Scott Highway and back to their homes.

2 **Add collective nouns** to these sentences.

a A ________________ of wild ducks flew over the dam.

b They saw the ________________ of lions in the shade.

c Did you see the ________________ of ships sail past?

3 **Circle** the **abstract nouns**. **Underline** the **verbal nouns**.

a Her love of animals was easily seen.

b May enjoyed galloping her pony across the plains.

c Parasailing brought her great enjoyment.

4 **Add noun groups** to **complete** the sentences.

a Many of ____________________________ played in the park.

b Did you see __________________________ at the fair?

5 **Circle** the **personal pronouns**, **underline** the **possessive pronouns** and **shade** the **reflexive pronouns**.

a Did you take your goods by yourself to his place?

b I know that the books are theirs.

6 **Circle** the **relative pronoun** in these sentences and **underline** the **adjectival clause**.

a Many of the animals escaped from the cages that were on the edge of the forest.

b Did you see the vehicle which belongs to Erica?

7 **Create** a **question** using the **interrogative pronouns** listed.

a (who) ____

b (what) ____

8 **Add** an **indefinite pronoun** to complete these sentences.

a Has __________________________ been able to find the bottle?

b __________________________ was ready for the party.

c There was __________________________ waiting at the gate.

9 **Circle** the **distributive pronouns** in these sentences.

a Each of the young girls enjoyed gymnastics.

b Did they visit either of the homes?

Answers on page 114

10 **Circle** the **numbering adjectives**. **Underline** the **descriptive adjectives**. **Shade** the **proper adjectives**.

a Seven of the tall ships were of Swedish origin while five were Dutch vessels.

b The largest vessel had blue funnels and its huge masts were made of fine English oak.

11 **Use** these **demonstrative adjectives** in short sentences.

a (those) ______________________________

b (that) ______________________________

12 **Insert** suitable **distributive adjectives** in these sentences.

a She saw ______________ car in the show.

b ______________ book was examined closely by the examiner.

13 **Identify** and **circle** the **indefinite adjectives** in these sentences.

a There were several animals in the yard.

b I saw some new trucks behind the sheds.

c Most modern homes have been built in this style.

14 Use these words as **interrogative adjectives** to **begin questions**.

a (what) ______________________________

b (whose) ______________________________

c (which) ______________________________

15 **Complete** these sentences using the **positive**, **comparative** or **superlative degree** of the **adjectives** in brackets.

a This rock is much (small) ______________ than the other one.

b Sharon has the (many) ______________ CDs of any of her classmates.

c Eric is always (careful) ______________ with his work than is his brother.

16 **Use** the **compound verb** *might be completed* in a sentence.

____

17 **Change** this sentence into the **future tense**.

They found the basket at the edge of the forest.

____

18 Are the verbs in these sentences **past tense**?

a He had played in the garden for hours. Yes ☐ No ☐ (*tick*)

b They collect the petals and place them in the basket. Yes ☐ No ☐

19 Write the **past tense**, **past participle** and **present participle** of these verbs.

a (choose) ______________ ______________ ______________

b (drive) ______________ ______________ ______________

☞ Answers on page 114

Adverbs – Common and interrogative

An **adverb** is a word that **describes** or **modifies other words** such as verbs, adjectives or other adverbs.

Common adverbs

Many adverbs tell **how** (manner), **when** (time) or **where** (place).

Examples

- The athlete ran **quickly**. (adverb telling **how** (manner), modifying the verb *ran*)
- The train arrived **late**. (adverb telling **when** (time), modifying the verb *arrived*)
- She went **there** yesterday. (adverb telling **where** (place), modifying the verb *went*)

1 **Underline** the adverbs telling **how**, **when** and **where**. **Write** *how*, *when* or *where* on the line.

a Karen began her work carefully. ____________

b The children will be asleep soon. ____________

c There on the shelf is the bottle. ____________

d Sue will visit the zoo later. ____________

e All the children were playing inside. ____________

2 **Use** these **adverbs** in suitable short sentences. **Underline** the words they **describe** or **modify**.

a angrily: ________________________________

b away: ________________________________

c soon: ________________________________

3 **Select** an **adverb** from the box to fit the spaces in these sentences.

a The rubbish was scattered ____________.

b Over and ____________ the drum rolled down the hill.

c ____________ I arose at six o'clock.

d The officer wanted the work done ____________.

e All the pieces of timber were lying ____________.

f Do you ____________ practise this instrument?

promptly	around	everywhere	over	yesterday	often

Interrogative adverbs

Interrogative adverbs are those that **begin questions**. They begin questions related to **how**, **when** or **where**.

Examples

- **Where** are you going? (adverb asking **where** or **what place**)
- **When** are you leaving? (adverb asking **when** or **what time**)
- **How** is it done correctly? (adverb asking **how** or **in what manner**)

4 **Add** an **interrogative adverb** to complete these questions.

a ____________ can I find the broken window?

b ____________ will the worker be finished?

c ____________ are you going to mend the vase?

Answers on page 115

Adverbs – Negative, numerical, of degree, describing, comparing

An **adverb** is a word that **describes** or **modifies other words** such as verbs, adjectives or other adverbs.

Negative adverbs

Negative adverbs create negative sentences. Two common negative adverbs are ***not*** and ***never***.

Examples

- He has **not** completed the work.
- She **never** travels to the country.

1 **Change** these sentences to negative sentences by adding a **negative adverb**.

a The boy has gone into the city. ________________

b She always collected the flowers in the garden. ________________

Numerical adverbs

Numerical adverbs indicate **how many times** an action takes place. Two numerical adverbs are ***twice*** and ***thrice***.

Examples

- She turned around **twice**.
- **Thrice** he knocked upon the door.

Adverbs of degree

Adverbs of degree indicate **to what extent** something is done or happens. Many of these adverbs really tell **how** something is done.

Examples

- The visitor was **really** wealthy.
- It was an **almost** unbeatable score.

2 **Circle** the adverbs of degree and **underline** the words they **describe** or **modify**.

a The young girl had been extremely sick.

b It was unbearably hot in the desert.

c She said it was nearly impossible to finish to task.

Comparing with adverbs

Adverbs can be used to **compare**.

Examples

- Jack ran **quickly**. (positive degree)
- Jack ran **quicker** than Jason. (comparative degree)
- Jack ran **quickest** of all. (superlative degree)

As with adjectives, if the **comparative** and **superlative degrees** of an **adverb** sound clumsy or awkward we add ***more*** or ***less*** for the **comparative** and ***most*** or ***least*** for the **superlative**.

3 **Complete** the table.

	Positive	Comparative	Superlative
a	near		
b	sadly		
c	dangerously		

☞ Answers on page 115

Adverbs

How much do you know?

1 **Insert** an **adverb** telling **how**, **when** or **where** in the spaces.

a Jae finished the race ________________.

b ________________ we will all go to the village.

c ________________ are many new kinds of plants.

d I do not know if they will go ________________.

e Some of the adults worked ________________.

2 **Use** these **adverbs** in suitable short sentences. **Underline** the words they **describe** or **modify**.

a noisily: ________________________________

b often: ________________________________

c outside: ________________________________

3 **Write** suitable **questions** beginning with these **interrogative adverbs**.

a how: ________________________________

b where: ________________________________

c when: ________________________________

4 Many **adverbs** are formed by adding ***-ly*** to an adjective. **Change** the word in **bold** into an **adverb**.

a He played a **smart** game. He played ________________.

b It was a **beautiful** gown. She was ________________ dressed.

c I heard the **noisy** party. They behaved ________________.

5 **Change** these sentences into negative sentences **using** a **negative adverb**.

a They did visit the spot. ________________________________

b I always see him.________________________________

6 **Select** the most suitable **adverb** of **degree** from the box for each of these sentences.

a The young boy was ______________________ careless with the work.

b She was ______________________ happy on her birthday.

c The rope was bound ______________________ around the parcel.

d He stood ______________________ close to the distressed patient.

tightly quite really comfortably

7 **Insert** the **correct degree** of **comparison** in these sentences.

a Colin arrived **early** to the meeting.

b John arrived ______________ than Joe did.

c Of all the children, Sue was the ________________ to arrive.

8 **Complete** the table.

	Positive	Comparative	Superlative
a	hard		
b	clumsily		

Answers on page 115

Conjunctions

A **conjunction** is a **joining word**. It **links together** single words, phrases and clauses.

Coordinating conjunctions

The most common **coordinating conjunctions** are ***and***, ***but*** and ***or***.

Examples

- Jack **and** Jo will leave for town.
- They were tired **but** delighted after the climb.
- Sharon **or** Lisa has been to the show.

(coordinating conjunctions joining single words)

- They played in the park **and** by the creek.
- She was in the water **or** on the boat.

(coordinating conjunctions joining phrases)

- He visited the spot **and** he found the lost bag.
- Tess collected the mail **or** she delivered the parcels every Tuesday.

(coordinating conjunctions joining clauses)

1 **Circle** the **coordinating conjunctions**. **Indicate** whether they are joining **single words**, **phrases** or **clauses**.

a Susie and Jim were at the party. ____________

b They will search in the shed or on the veranda. ____________

c He worked hard but he was very tired. ____________

2 **Add** suitable **coordinating conjunctions** to these incomplete sentences.

a They washed the car ____________ did not do it well.

b Sacha ____________ Lyn will collect the parcel.

c Sam ____________ his brother Brad were in the event.

Subordinating conjunctions

Subordinating conjunctions join **two** or **more clauses**. One is the **main clause** (**principal clause**) and the others are **subordinate clauses** (often **adverbial clauses**).

Examples

- Heather will leave **when** the work is complete.
- They will not finish it **unless** they hurry.
- Rod left **because** he was sick.

3 **Circle** the **subordinating conjunctions** in these sentences.

a The visitors will go after the dance is over.

b He ran well though he did not win.

c She will paint the fence today if she is allowed.

Pairs of conjunctions

Sometimes **conjunctions work** in **pairs** to join words, phrases or clauses.

Examples

- **Neither** Tom **nor** his brother attended the camp.
- They left **as** soon **as** they could.

4 **Circle** the **conjunction pairs** in these sentences.

a Either Elaine or David will wait at the gate.

b Both horse and rider were injured in the fall.

c Not one but two shells could be seen.

☞ Answers on page 115

Prepositions and interjections

Prepositions

A **preposition** is a word that **begins** a **phrase**. It usually has a **noun** or **pronoun** after it.

to	in	of	up	with	over	around	among
at	on	by	across	from	into	after	between

Examples

- The little kitten ran **up** the curtain.
- She looked at the painting **on** the wall.
- The horse galloped **over** the road and **into** the paddock.

1 **Circle** the **prepositions** in these sentences and **underline** the **phrases** they begin.

- **a** All of the students travelled to the farm by the lake.
- **b** The animals came from the zoos over the mountains.
- **c** Past the yard and along the fence they raced.

2 **Add** suitable **prepositions** to these incomplete sentences.

- **a** The box was __________ the drawer __________ the filing cabinet.
- **b** __________ the leaves she found the book __________ a faded cover.
- **c** She gazed __________ the statue __________ amazement.

Some words are used as **prepositions** and as **adverbs**.

Examples

- Many of the recruits walked **by**. (**adverb** telling where)
- The house was built **by** the creek. (**preposition** beginning phrase)
- The raging waters surged **beneath**. (**adverb** telling where)
- She sat **beneath** the bridge. (**preposition** beginning phrase)

3 **State** whether the words in **bold** are **adverbs (A)** or **prepositions (P)**.

- **a** The children played **around**. __________
- **b** **Around** the yard the dog ran happily. __________
- **c** Do not go **down** the road. __________
- **d** **Down** he fell from a great height. __________

4 Use *after* in one sentence as an **adverb** and in another as a **preposition**.

- **a** (as adverb) ______________________________
- **b** (as preposition) ______________________________

Interjections

Interjections are usually short words that express **sudden feeling**. They are followed by an **exclamation mark (!)**.

5 **Underline** the **interjections** in these sentences.

- **a** Wow! That was an excellent movie.
- **b** Oh! I'm sorry about that.
- **c** Ouch! That really hurts.
- **d** Bravo! What a great win they had.

Answers on page 115

Section test 1B

1 **Select** an **adverb** from the box to fit the spaces in these sentences.

a The aircraft flew ________________.

b She spoke ________________ to the disobedient child.

c All the people walked ________________ up the hill.

d She said it was a ________________ good film.

e Did the dog run ________________ yesterday?

f At the shelter the travellers rested ________________.

very	above	quietly	slowly	angrily	away

2 **Use these adverbs** in short sentences. **Underline** the words they **describe** or **modify**.

a soon: ____

b hugely: ____

c often: ____

3 **Add** suitable **interrogative adverbs** to **complete** these questions.

a ________________ did you find the small ball?

b ________________ can you finish the task?

c ________________ are you taking the parcel?

4 **Change** these sentences into negative sentences **using** a **negative adverb**.

a Harriet has left for her music lesson.

____

b Craig always washes the car on Sunday.

____

5 **Circle** the **adverbs** of **degree** and **underline** the words they **describe** or **modify**.

a The boy worked too quickly.

b The time was almost five o'clock.

c Much of the work was partly finished.

6 **Add** suitable **adverbs telling** us **how**.

a The soldiers advanced ________________ through the desert.

b All the refugees were trudging ________________ to the border gate.

c This old book needs to be treated ________________.

d It was damaged ________________ in the flood.

e The visitors smiled ________________ at the entertainers.

7 **Insert** the **correct degree** of **comparison** in these sentences.

a The parcel was **tightly** packed.

b This parcel was ________________ packed than the other.

c This was the ________________ packed parcel of all.

Answers on page 115

Section test 1B

8 **Use coordinating conjunctions** to **complete** these sentences.

- **a** Sarah ________________ Jodie attended the event.
- **b** The boys ________________ girls have been there many times.
- **c** She went reluctantly ________________ did not enjoy it.

9 **Circle** the **coordinating conjunctions** and **underline** the **words**, **phrases** or **clauses** they join.

- **a** In the evening and at sunrise they visited the lake.
- **b** His brother Steve or his cousin Ray played in the team.
- **c** She returned the book but she had not finished reading it.

10 **Circle** the **subordinating conjunctions**.

- **a** All the relatives left after the party was finished.
- **b** She travelled alone wherever she could.
- **c** It was not built because the rain was too heavy.

11 **Use** the word *if* as a **subordinating conjunction joining two clauses**.

____

____

12 **Use** this **conjunction pair** in a suitable sentence: *not … but*.

____

____

13 **Circle** the **prepositions** and **underline** the **phrases** they begin.

- **a** They went to the shop in the afternoon.
- **b** They searched by night for the missing dog.
- **c** Near the stable and beyond the water trough they traced the footprints.

14 **Add** suitable **prepositions** to these incomplete sentences.

- **a** They left either ____________ the morning or ____________ night.
- **b** ____________ the mountains a lake could be seen.
- **c** Some ____________ the teams were training ____________ the old hut.

15 **State** whether the words in **bold** are **adverbs** or **prepositions**.

- **a** They searched **around** for several hours. ________________
- **b** Do not come **near**. ________________
- **c** This saddle was **near** the feed bin. ________________
- **d** They stopped **before** the town. ________________
- **e** Did he just leave **before**? ________________

16 **Circle** the **interjections** in these sentences.

- **a** Eek! What a terrible mess.
- **b** Oops! I have dropped the plate.
- **c** Hush! You'll wake the young children.

Answers on pages 115–116

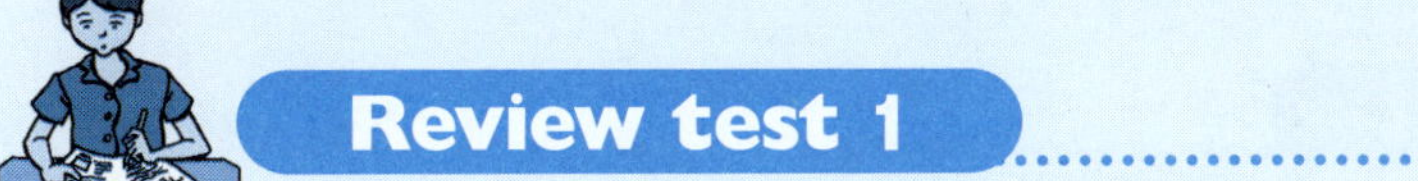

Review test 1

1 **Add nouns** of the **type indicated** to **complete** these sentences.

a The (common) ____________ enjoyed a game in (proper) ____________ Park.

b During the month of (proper) ____________ the (proper) ____________ family went to the (common) ____________.

c The (collective) ____________ of (common) ____________ played the game in (proper) ____________.

d The (abstract) ____________ and (abstract) ____________ were shown clearly on their faces.

2 **Circle** the **verbal nouns** in these sentences.

a She enjoys riding her new pony.

b Collecting the football cards was a good hobby.

c By cultivating the field well, the farmer hoped for a good crop.

3 **Add** a **noun group** of **at least four words** to these sentences.

a The ______________________________ moved slowly down the road.

b Did you notice ______________________________?

c Some of ______________________________ were employed.

4 **List four nouns** beginning with the letter ***b***. Include a **common noun**, **proper noun**, **collective noun** and **abstract noun**.

____

5 **Add pronouns** of the **type indicated** to **complete** these sentences.

a (personal) ____________ gave it back because it was (possessive) ____________.

b Are (possessive) ____________ cousins visiting (personal) ____________?

c Liz played by (reflexive) ____________ in the sand pit.

d This is the car (relative) ____________ was broken down.

e (interrogative) ____________ is going to the show with you?

f (indefinite) ____________ items were left on the floor.

g (demonstrative) ____________ is a very attractive painting.

h (distributive) ____________ of the boats was repaired.

6 **Create** a **sentence** using *that* as a **relative pronoun**.

____

7 **Colour** the **numbering adjectives** red, **descriptive adjectives** green, **proper adjectives** blue and **demonstrative adjectives** yellow.

a Nine yachts sailed into the deep blue harbour.

b The Russian aircraft landed at Mascot airport.

c This green vehicle collected the large American container.

8 Are the **adjectives** in **bold distributive** or **indefinite** adjectives?

a **Each** animal was housed in a clean stall. ____________

b They collected **many** presents. ____________

Answers on page 116

9 **Create** a **sentence** beginning with the **interrogative adjective** *what*.

____

10 **Complete** the sentences using the **comparative** and **superlative degree** of the **adjective** in the first sentence.

a Linda is **careful** with her work.

b Duncan is ______________________ than Linda with his work.

c Of all the children William is the ______________________.

11 **Write** a **sentence** using this **compound verb**: *has been repairing*.

____

12 **Rewrite** this sentence in the **future tense**: The mechanic adjusted the brakes.

____

13 **Add** suitable **participles** to these incomplete sentences.

a The worker had ______________ the side of the house.

b Have you been ______________ all the paths?

c The hall was ______________ from a great height.

14 **Circle** the **infinitives** in these sentences.

a Here is a new book to read.

b She attended the concert to hear her favourite singer.

15 **Underline** the **adverbs** in these sentences. **Indicate** whether they tell us **how**, **when** or **where**.

a She will visit the store later in the day. ______________

b They sang cheerfully during the evening. ______________

c Do not go there for some time. ______________

16 **Circle** the **adverbs** of **degree**. **Underline** the words they **describe** or **modify**.

a He was quite ill late last week.

b It has been terribly windy during the past few days.

17 **Create two sentences**, one containing a **coordinating conjunction** and the other a **subordinating conjunction**.

a ____

b ____

18 **Write** a **sentence** including these three **prepositions**: *above*, *on*, *at*.

____

19 Is the word in **bold** in this sentence an **adverb**?

Many of them fell **below**. Yes ☐ No ☐ *(tick)*

20 Use the interjection *Ah!* correctly **in** a **sentence**.

____

☞ Answers on page 116

2 Sentence parts and features

Sentence parts – Subject

A **sentence** is a **group** of **words** with a **verb** included.

A sentence can be divided into two parts: one part is called the **subject**. To find the subject, you must **first find** the **verb**.

Example

- Rose painted the mural.
  What is the verb? The verb is *painted*.
  To find the subject, ask this question: *Who or what painted?*
  Rose painted, so *Rose* is the **subject**.

The **subject** can be:

- **left out altogether** or **'understood'** if the verb is a command or order
- a **single noun** or **pronoun**
- **several nouns** or **pronouns** and **other groups** of **words**.

Examples

- Hurry. (verb) (This really means 'you' hurry. The subject **you** is understood.)
- **Edward** (subject) collected (verb) the money.
- **Bill, Alex and their brothers** (subject) are (verb) here.

1 **Circle** the **verb**. **Underline** the **subject**.

a Many of the boys collected the keys.

b Some friends of ours are building a house nearby.

c The scientist studied the small creatures.

2 **Select** a suitable **subject** from the box to **complete** these sentences.

All the animals	The tall giraffe	The garbage truck
The police officers	My young sister	

a ______________________ found the car by the river.

b ______________________ had taken it all away.

c ______________________ wrote the letter last week.

The **subject** is **not always** at the **beginning** of a sentence.

Example

- Where are **you** going? (are going is the verb. Who or what are going? **You** is the subject.)

3 **Circle** the **verbs** and **underline** the **subjects**.

a Which dress will Karen be wearing?

b Beneath the reef the young girl swam.

c Which type of vehicle will Bob select?

Answers on page 116

Sentence parts – Predicate

A **sentence** can be divided into **two parts**. One part is called the **subject** and the other is called the **predicate**. The **verb** is included in the **predicate**.

Example

- The young boys lived in the country.
  What is the verb? *lived*
  Who or what lived? *The young boys* (subject)
  The **predicate** is *lived in the country*.

1 **Circle** the **verbs**. Ask the question to find the subject.
Underline the **predicate**. **Hint:** Don't forget to include the verb.

a Many of the homes were damaged by the hail.
b Several children attended the meeting yesterday.
c The new foals were placed in the paddock.
d A smart new canoe was made by the boys.
e The office furniture was left in storage.

2 **Select** suitable **predicates** from the box for these sentences.

in Crown Street	grazing in the paddock	rushed wildly away
damaged yesterday	a diamond ring near the gate	

a The children found ______________________.
b Some of the cows were ______________________.
c The girl in the blue dress lives ______________________.

3 **Complete** these sentences by adding a **verb** and the rest of the **predicate**. **Underline** the **verb**.

a My cousin Elle ______________________________________.
b The ladder ______________________________________.
c The boys ______________________________________.

The **predicate** does **not** always have to be at the **end** of a **sentence**.

Examples

- What is he doing there?
  The verb = *is doing*. The subject = *he*. The predicate = *is doing what there*.
- Across the glassy lake, the champion skaters moved.
  The verb = *moved*. The subject = *the champion skaters*. The predicate = *moved across the glassy lake*.

4 **Circle** the **verb** and **underline** the **predicates** in these sentences.

a Has she been working here all day?
b Near the lake by the homestead the animals grazed.
c Where can we find a glue stick?
d Down from the bridge the foaming water rushed wildly.

Answers on page 116

Sentence parts – Direct object

A sentence may contain an **object**. An **object** of a **sentence** is the person or thing **acted on** by the **subject**. It is called a **direct object**.

Example

- She bought a bag of cherries.
  The verb = *bought*. The subject = *she*.
  To find the **direct object**, ask this question: *Who or what did she buy?* The **direct object** = *a bag of cherries*.

To **frame** the **question** to find the object, you must use the **subject** and the **verb**: *Who or what did (subject) (verb)?*

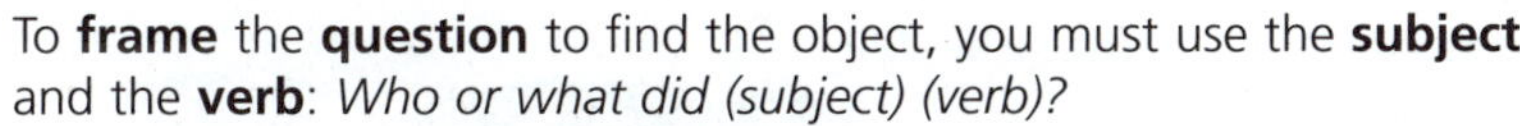

1 **Circle** the **verbs**. Find the subject and ask the question. **Underline** the **object**.

a Miriam recognised her cousin immediately.
b My young brother collects stamps.
c The large truck carried its load to the village.
d The tribe hunted the bison in summer.
e Petros and Toko studied that subject last year.

2 **Circle** the **verbs**. Complete the sentence by **adding** a **suitable object**.

a Kim was carrying ______________________ to the classroom.
b The youngster had eaten ______________________ in a flash.
c These people saw ______________________ at the gate yesterday.

Not every sentence has an **object**. The sentence only has an object if there is an answer to the question: *What did (subject) (verb)?*

Example

- The wild dogs barked loudly.
  The verb = *barked*. The subject = *the wild dogs*. What did the wild dogs bark? There is no answer, so there is no object.

3 Do these sentences have objects? **Answer yes** or **no** and **underline** the **object**.

a The officer shouted the instructions. Yes ☐ No ☐ *(tick)*
b The officer shouted at the troops. Yes ☐ No ☐
c Mary studied the work very well. Yes ☐ No ☐
d Mary studied in the evenings. Yes ☐ No ☐

4 Do these sentences have objects? **Answer yes or no** and **underline the object**.

a Did she import the car from America? Yes ☐ No ☐ *(tick)*
b Was it captured very easily? Yes ☐ No ☐
c A beautiful ballad she sang so well. Yes ☐ No ☐
d Did the girl catch the ball? Yes ☐ No ☐

Answers on page 116

Sentence parts – Indirect object

A **direct object** of a sentence is the **person** or **thing acted on** by the **subject**. An **indirect object** is the **person** or **thing** who **received** the **direct object**.

Example

- Rachel gave the book to her friend.
  What is the verb? *gave*
  What did Rachel give? *the book* (direct object)
  To whom did she give the book? *her friend* (**indirect object**)
  The friend is the person to whom Rachel (subject) gave (verb) the book (direct object).

1 **Circle** the **direct objects** and **underline** the **indirect objects**.

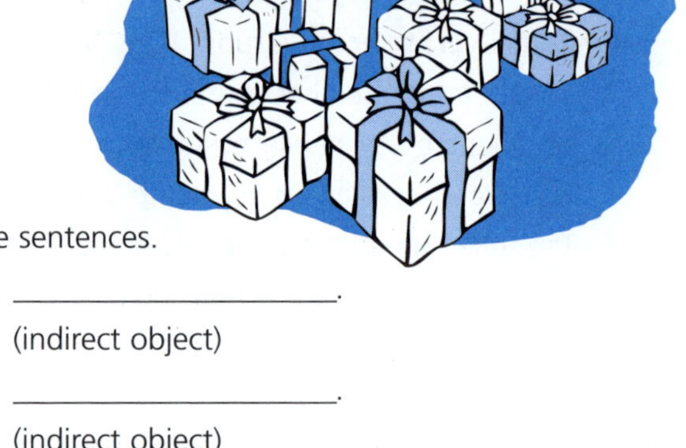

- **a** Jim had posted the letter to his father.
- **b** They gave the presents to Nina.
- **c** They all brought the drinks to Ellen.
- **d** The children passed the bucket to Ken.
- **e** Georgia sent a brand new watch to her sister.

2 **Add** suitable **direct** and **indirect objects** to these sentences.

- **a** They mailed ____________________ ______________________.
  (direct object) (indirect object)
- **b** Ken handed the ____________________ ______________________.
  (direct object) (indirect object)
- **c** They passed the ____________________ ______________________.
  (direct object (indirect object)

In many sentences, the word *to* is **in front of** the **indirect object**, but not always. Sometimes *to* is left out.

Example

- Sue gave me five dollars.
  What is the verb? *gave*
  What is the subject? *Sue*
  What did Sue give? *five dollars* (direct object)
  To whom did Sue give five dollars? *me* (indirect object—the word *to* has been left out)

3 **Circle** the **direct objects** and **underline** the **indirect objects**.

- **a** The children in this class mailed Sam a new toy.
- **b** All the adults showed the girls the new costumes.
- **c** They posted him the small package.

4 **Add direct** and **indirect objects** to these sentences.

- **a** The young sailor handed ________________ ______________________.
  (indirect object) (direct object)
- **b** Many of the students brought ______________ ______________________.
  (indirect object) (direct object)

Answers on pages 116–117

Sentence parts – Complement

Complements are found in sentences with **being verbs**.

The **being verb** links the **subject** and the **complement**.

Example

- The young boy (subject) became (being verb) a sailor. (complement)

  The verb *became* **links** the **subject** to the **complement**. The *boy* and the *sailor* are the **same**.

1 **Underline** the **verbs** and **circle** the **complements**.

a His favourite pet is his Labrador dog.

b My greatest friends are Jim and Jae.

c This vegetable is a zucchini.

d I am an electrician.

2 **Select** suitable **complements** from the box to complete these sentences.

a very talented artist	my sister	a howling gale
many more horses	last but not least	a favourite with local gardeners

a This particular plant is ____________________.

b Catherine was ____________________.

c The gentle breeze later became ____________________.

d This girl is ____________________.

3 **Select** suitable **subjects** from the box to complete these sentences. **Underline** the **complement**.

The animals on the move	After a year	The African prince
Several	Our next door neighbour	A constant companion

a ____________________ was a proud warrior.

b ____________________ is a very successful writer.

c ____________________ were migrating caribou.

In all the sentences above, the complements were nouns.

Sometimes the **complement** can be **one** or **more adjectives**.

Example

- The girl (subject) was (being verb) happy and bright. (complement)

  The adjectives *happy* and *bright* are describing the girl.

  The sentence could be written as *The girl was a happy and bright girl*.

  The adjectives *happy* and *bright* make up the **complement**.

4 **Underline** the **subjects** and **circle** the **complements**.

a The speech was long and boring.

b This room is untidy.

c The brilliant light became dull and yellow.

Answers on page 117

Section test 2A

1 **Circle** the **verb** and **underline** the **subject**.

a Some of the visitors brought the presents.

b All of the lecturers taught at the college.

c This excellent crop was grown in the Taryn Valley.

d I have found many of them.

e The building with the wide staircase is on the corner.

2 **Add** suitable **subjects** to these sentences.

a ______________________ will be able to finish the task.

b ______________________ had taken it away.

c ______________________ began to leave the office.

3 **Circle** the **verbs** and **underline** the **subjects**.

a Which machine will you use?

b Under the wreck the divers swam easily.

c What subject are you studying there?

4 **Circle** the **verbs** and **underline** the **rest** of the **predicate**.

a A flight of birds flew over the swamp.

b Many workers remained in the paddocks.

c The recently painted house was sold last week.

d All of the artists gathered at the display centre.

e My cousin Jess lives in Greer Street.

5 **Add** suitable **predicates** to these sentences.

a The old man ____.

b Several pioneers ____.

c His nephew Matt ____.

6 **Circle** the **verbs** and **underline** the **rest** of the **predicates**.

a Have they been packing up all the year?

b By the stream across the valley they travelled.

c What can the student see on the horizon?

7 Use this group of words as a **subject** in a **sentence**.

The herd of cattle

____

8 Use this group of words as a **predicate** in a **sentence**.

recognised the spot easily

____

9 **Circle** the **verbs**. **Underline** the **subject**. Frame the question and **shade the object**.

a The weary travellers collected their luggage.

b His elder sister enjoys basketball.

c Some of the team tidied the area well.

Answers on page 117

Section test 2A

10 **Circle** the **verbs**. **Underline** the **subject**. Complete the sentences by **adding** a suitable **direct object**.

- **a** The girl was taking ______________________ to the library.
- **b** All the children admired ______________________.
- **c** The student glued ______________________.

11 Do these sentences have **direct objects**? Answer **yes** or **no** and **underline** the **object**.

a	The equipment was left in the field.	Yes ☐	No ☐	*(tick)*
b	Did the company export tractor parts?	Yes ☐	No ☐	
c	A delightful poem she created so easily.	Yes ☐	No ☐	
d	There was not a plate on the table.	Yes ☐	No ☐	

12 Use this group of words as a **direct object** in a **sentence**.

a box of supplies ____.

13 **Circle** the **direct objects** and **underline** the **indirect objects**.

- **a** She gave the package to Kristy.
- **b** The soldier brought the weapon to Sergeant Ellis.
- **c** They passed the broom to her.
- **d** Aunt Lucy sent a fine new painting to her.
- **e** Jake has not given it to me.

14 **Circle** the **direct objects** and **underline** the **indirect objects**.

- **a** The teacher gave me a new manuscript.
- **b** Many of the scientists showed the people the experiment.
- **c** His sister posted him a new tie.

15 **Add direct** and **indirect objects** to these sentences.

- **a** My cousin Joe gave ________________ (indirect) ________________ (direct).
- **b** Some of his classmates brought ________________ (indirect) ________________ (direct).

16 **Underline** the **verbs** and **circle** the **complements**.

- **a** My best painting is that portrait.
- **b** Jim's best friends are Steve and Liam.
- **c** Joy is a research scientist.
- **d** The small pony became the thoroughbred's companion.
- **e** Those dying plants were once fine roses.

17 **Add** suitable **complements** to **complete** these sentences.

- **a** Many of the visitors were ______________________.
- **b** The old sailor was ______________________.
- **c** The athlete became ______________________.

☞ Answers on page 117

Features – Person

Person is a feature of **personal pronouns** and **nouns**.
There are **three persons: first**, **second** and **third**.

The **actual persons speaking** are called **first person**.

Examples

- **I** am going to the show. (The pronoun *I* is first person.)
- **We** will collect the parcels. (The pronoun *we* is first person.)

The **persons being spoken to** are called **second person**.

Example

- **You** are not driving the car. (The pronoun *You* is second person.)

Most **nouns** and some **pronouns** are called **third person**.

Example

- The **car** is at the **gate**. (*car* and *gate* = third person.)

1 **Underline** the **first person pronouns** and **circle** the **second person pronouns**.

a We will take the horse to the track.

b I think that you should work harder.

c This is ours and does this belong to you?

2 Add **first person** and **second person pronouns** to **complete** these sentences.

a ____________ (1st) have not seen ____________ (2nd) there before.

b ____________ (1st) asked you is this ____________ (2nd).

c Have ____________ (2nd) collected it for ____________ (1st) yet?

3 Are the pronouns in **bold first**, **second** or **third person**?

a The girl saw **it** on the oval. ____________

b I told **you** to complete the work. ____________

c Do not give that to **me**. ____________

Most nouns are **third person** but here are **two exceptions**.

Examples

- We, **the Johnsons**, lived in Willow Street.
  We and *the Johnsons* = the same people, so *the Johnsons* = first person.
- **Sharon**, you have won the prize.
  Sharon and *you* = the same person, so *Sharon* = second person.

4 **Indicate** whether the **nouns** and **pronouns** in the sentences below are **first**, **second** or **third person**.

a She (____) is going with her (____) brother (____).

b Will you (____) give it (____) to him (____)?

c Paula (____), you (____) will carry the flag (____).

Answers on page 117

Features – Number

Number is a feature of **nouns** and **pronouns**.

- If the **noun** or **pronoun stands for one thing**, it is called a **singular noun**.
- If the **noun** or **pronoun stands for more than one thing**, it is called a **plural noun**.

Example

- **They** took **me** to the **concerts** in the **park**.
  (plural) (singular) (plural) (singular)

1 **Write** (**S**) for singular or (**P**) for plural in the boxes below the words in **bold**.

a **My** **father** took **us** with **him** to the **beach**.
☐ ☐ ☐ ☐ ☐

b This **animal** was fed by **them** in the **house** over the **road**.
☐ ☐ ☐ ☐

c **Our cousins** visited **us** during the last two **weeks** of **May**.
☐ ☐ ☐ ☐ ☐

2 Add a **noun** or **pronoun** of the **number indicated** to complete these sentences.

a This (S) ______________ was taken to the (S) ______________ for a (S) ______________.

b The (P) ______________ on the (S) ______________ had been collected by the (P) ______________.

c (S) ______________, (S) ______________ and (S) ______________ went to the (P)______________ every (S)______________.

Rules

If the **subject** of a sentence is **singular**, the **verb form must be singular**.

- The **boy are working** in the shop. INCORRECT
- The **boy is working** in the shop. CORRECT

If the **subject** of a sentence **is plural**, the **verb** form **must be plural**.

- The **girls was playing** in the yard. INCORRECT
- The **girls were playing** in the yard. CORRECT

3 Use the two rules to **correct these sentences** by **altering** the **verb**.

a Several boys is collecting the mail.

____

b The bright young girl are riding along the road.

____

c A small object were seen across the beach.

____

d The car and the truck was on the ferry.

____

☞ Answers on page 117

Features – Gender

Gender is a feature of **nouns** and **pronouns**.

There are **four genders**:

- **Masculine**: male persons or animals (e.g. *man*, *prince*, *stallion*)
- **Feminine**: female persons or animals (e.g. *woman*, *princess*, *mare*)
- **Common**: either male or female (e.g. *child*, *adult*, *cattle*)
- **Neuter**: neither male nor female (e.g. *road*, *bottle*, *cupboard*)

1 **Circle** the **masculine** nouns and pronouns and **underline** the **feminine** nouns and pronouns.

- **a** His grandmother took the hostess to the party.
- **b** The young lad went with his niece to his uncle's home.
- **c** The wife of the hero in the story lived in that castle.

2 **Circle** the **common nouns** and **underline** the **neuter nouns** in these sentences.

- **a** As the boat approached the children swam away.
- **b** The cattle and sheep were loaded into the truck.
- **c** My friend went on holidays with some of her classmates.

3 Draw lines to **match** the **masculine** and **feminine forms** of these nouns.

baron	bride
boar	cow
bridegroom	duck
brother	duchess
bull	sister
drake	sow
fox	baroness
gander	filly
duke	goose
colt	vixen

4 Insert a **pronoun** of **masculine** or **feminine gender** to complete these sentences.

- **a** The countess went with ____________ cousin to visit the emperor at ____________ palace.
- **b** My grandfather took ____________ grandson with ____________ to buy ____________ a new bicycle.
- **c** Although the heroine escaped from ____________ captor ____________ still had to rescue the other child.

The **pronoun** must be of the **same gender** as the **noun** it stands for.

Example

- As the **tiger** came close, **her** injured paw could be seen. INCORRECT
  Tiger = masculine, so the pronoun *her* should be *his*.

5 **Circle** the **incorrect pronoun** and **write** the **correct pronoun** at the end of the sentence.

- **a** The mare snorted loudly and stamped his feet. ________________
- **b** My niece keeps his horse in that paddock. ________________
- **c** The sow was looking after his litter. ________________

Answers on pages 117–118

Section test 2B

1 **Underline** the **first person pronouns** and **circle** the **second person pronouns**.

a I will take you with me to his place.

b We read your note last week.

c These are yours but this one is ours.

2 **Underline** the **second person pronouns** and **circle** the **third person nouns**.

a Is this your new bag on the table?

b My cousin Alan collected that bike of yours.

c Has the cage been cleaned by the workers?

3 **Indicate** whether the words in **bold** are **first**, **second** or **third person**.

a **Brad**, **you** cannot take that away. __________ __________

b **We**, the **Adams**, would like to visit your farm. __________ __________

4 **Correct** these sentences by **altering** the **verb** so that the **subject** and **verb** are **matched correctly**.

a She are going away. ______________________________

b Were he there? ______________________________

c My cousin and I is going. ______________________________

5 Enter (**S**) for singular or (**P**) for plural in the boxes below the words in **bold**.

a **Our mothers** collected **her books** from the **library**.

☐ ☐ ☐ ☐ ☐

b The **goats** and the **chickens** were left in **their paddock** for at least a **week**.

☐ ☐ ☐ ☐ ☐

c Several **shots** were fired by the **farmer** behind the **sheds** near the **creek**.

☐ ☐ ☐ ☐

6 Use these combinations to **create sentences**.

a *his* (third person, singular number), *vehicles* (third person, plural number)

____

b *your* (second person, singular number), *parcel* (third person, singular number)

____

7 **Add** a **noun** or **pronoun** of the **number indicated** to **complete** these sentences.

a The (S) ________________ was taken to the (P) ________________ at the end of the (S) ________________.

b My young (P) ______________ have always collected the (P) ______________ from the (S) ________________ next to the new (P) ________________.

☞ Answers on page 118

8 **Correct** these sentences by **altering** the **verb**.

a Groups of boys and girls was playing in the yard.

____

b That painter were employed by the company.

____

c The boat and the trailer was by the creek.

____

9 **Circle** the **masculine** nouns and pronouns and **underline** the **feminine** nouns and pronouns in these sentences.

a Joan sees him after and borrows books from him.

b Paolo will meet his friend Gretel and they will eat at the local cafe.

c Mother supplies his shop with material which she weaves herself.

10 Rewrite these sentences **changing** the **gender** of each of the nouns in **bold**.

a The **mayor** and the **manager** drove their **wives** to the theatre.

____

b My **aunt** went with my **niece** to see the movie.

____

c The **groomsman** and the **groom** arrived early.

____

d The **man's son** helped to load the **heifer** and the **ewe** into the wagon.

____

11 Write the **feminine gender** of the following.

a master _______________ b lad _______________

c ram _______________ d priest _______________

e widower _______________ f prince _______________

12 Use this combination to **create** a **new sentence**: a **third person**, **singular number**, **masculine gender noun** AND a **first person**, **plural number pronoun**.

____

____

Answers on page 118

Features – Nominative case

Case is a feature of **nouns** and **pronouns**. It is the **relationship** between these nouns and pronouns and **other words** in a **sentence**.

Nominative case means to do with the **subject** or the **complement**.

Examples

- The car was on the lawn.
  What is the verb? *was* What is the subject? *The car*
  The car = the whole subject, but the **key subject word** or **simple subject** = *car*.
  The word *car* is said to be **nominative case subject** of the verb *was*.
- He worked well.
  What is the verb? *worked* What is the subject? *He*
  The pronoun *He* = nominative case.

Personal pronouns, nominative case

I	you	he	they
we	she	it	

1 **Circle** the **verb** and **underline** the **simple subjects**.

a The old man lived in the hut.

b The young children have played there many times.

c All my friends helped me yesterday.

2 **Add** a suitable noun or pronoun that is **nominative case subject** of the **verb** to these sentences.

a The bright yellow ____________________ rounded the bend.

b His favourite ____________________ stood on the table.

c The large dark ____________________ stretched across the sky.

3 **Circle** the **verb** and **underline** the word that is **nominative case subject** of the **verb**.

a Across the plain the stallion galloped rapidly.

b Near the wharf was a large rat.

c There is the building with a red roof.

The **key word** in the **complement** of a sentence is also nominative case but is described as **nominative case complement** of the **verb**.

Example

- The girl became captain of the netball team.
  girl = **nominative case subject** of the verb *became*
  captain = **nominative case complement** of the verb *became*

4 **Underline** the **verb**. **Circle** the word that is **nominative case complement** of the **verb**.

a I am his loyal friend.

b Isla and Shaun are good workers.

c Is that the correct path to town?

5 **Write** a **sentence** using the word *question* as **nominative case complement** of a **verb**.

____

____

☞ Answers on page 118

Features – Objective case (verb, preposition)

Case is a feature of **nouns** and **pronouns**. It is the **relationship** between these nouns and pronouns and **other words** in a **sentence**.

Objective case means to do with the **object**.

Example

- She took the parcel to the shop.

What is the verb?	*took*
What is the subject?	*She*
What did she take?	*the parcel* (direct object)

parcel is **objective case governed** by the **verb** *took*.
Now look at the group of words *to the shop*. *to* is a **preposition**. It **governs** *shop*.
shop is **objective case governed** by the **preposition** *to*.

Personal pronouns, objective case

me you us her him it them

1 **Circle** the **verb** and **underline** the **direct object**.

a The boy found the shiny coin.

b Several of the students failed the test.

c The tall woman has collected large paintings.

2 **Add** a suitable noun or pronoun that is **objective case governed** by the **verb**.

a Matilda had seen ____________ by the lake.

b Many children played ____________________.

c This new machine produces __________________ every minute.

3 **Circle** the **verb** and **underline** the word that is **objective case governed** by the **verb**.

a Has the boy delivered the letters?

b My young brother collects stamps as a hobby.

c The old piece of machinery developed engine problems.

4 **Circle** the **preposition** and **underline** the word that is **objective case governed** by the **preposition**.

a Many players rested in the shade.

b At the fence were the young people.

c Have you been to his house lately?

5 Complete these sentences by **adding nouns**. **Underline** the word that is **objective case governed** by the **preposition**.

a The villagers raced to ____________________________________.

b Some of __________________________ had been there many times.

c All the animals grazed in ______________________________.

Quick check

Circle the words that are **objective case governed** by the **verb**. **Underline** the words that are **objective case governed** by a **preposition**.

1 My young sister found the pegs near the mailbox.

2 At noon all of the farmers delivered the produce.

Answers on page 118

Features – Objective case (infinitive, verbal noun, participle)

Case is a feature of **nouns** and **pronouns**. It is the **relationship** between these nouns and pronouns and **other words** in a **sentence**.

Objective case means to do with the **object**.

Infinitive

Example

- She went to buy the apples.
  What is the infinitive? *to buy* What did she buy? *apples*
  apples = **objective case governed** by the **infinitive** *to buy*.

1 **Circle** the **infinitives** and **underline** the word that is **objective case governed** by the **infinitive**.

a My brother will try to sell the car.

b To eat the green fruit was almost impossible.

c The musician began to play a lilting melody.

2 **Add** a suitable noun or pronoun that is **objective case governed** by an **infinitive**.

a They all went to play ____________________.

b Have the workers begun to mend ____________________.

c All the students tried to complete ____________________.

Nouns or pronouns can also be **objective case governed** by a **verbal noun**.

Verbal noun

Example

- The boy was fond of collecting shells.
  What is the verbal noun? *collecting*. What was he fond of collecting? *shells*
  shells = **objective case governed** by the **verbal noun** *collecting*.

3 **Circle** the **verbal nouns** and **underline** the words that are **objective case governed** by the **verbal noun**.

a Ian always enjoyed playing the piano.

b The young colts loved chasing the ponies.

c Planting the first trees was the next task.

4 **Add** a suitable noun or pronoun and **underline** the word that is **objective case governed** by the **verbal noun**.

a Megan disliked weeding the ____________________.

b Collecting the ____________________ was his favourite hobby.

Participle

Nouns or pronouns can also be **objective case governed** by a **participle**.

Example

- Peta is the girl riding the horse. *horse* = **objective case governed** by the **participle** *riding*.

5 **Circle** the **participles** and **underline** the words that are **objective case governed** by the **participle**.

a The boy collecting the mail is my brother.

b The child eating the fruit is in my class.

c The worker painting the fence is an apprentice.

Answers on page 118

Features – Possessive case

Case is a feature of **nouns** and **pronouns**. It is the **relationship** between these nouns and pronouns and **other words** in a **sentence**.

Possessive case indicates **ownership**.

Example

- Maddie's horse is in the paddock.
  Who owns the horse? *Maddie* (The apostrophe shows ownership.)
  Maddie's = **possessive case** owning **horse**.

Possessive pronouns

mine ours yours hers his theirs its

1 **Circle** the nouns that are **possessive case** and **underline** the noun that is **owned**.

a The girls' clothes are in the bag.

b Have the children's books been corrected yet?

c Rosie's golf shoes were in the cupboard.

d I was introduced to Mr Wong's cousins.

e Heath's friends had been with him at the show.

2 **Add** a **noun**, **possessive case**, and an **item** that is **owned**.

a This is ____________________________________.

b Can all of you see ____________________________________?

c ______________________________ had been left on the veranda.

Apostrophe

The apostrophe is used to indicate **possession**.

The apostrophe can be placed either **before** or **after** the ***s***.

Examples

- The **girl's uniform** has been ironed.
  girl's = **possessive case** owning *uniform*.
  One girl (singular number) means the **apostrophe** is placed **before** the ***s***.
- The five **girls' uniforms** have been ironed.
  girls' = **possessive case** owning *uniforms*.
  Several girls (plural) means the **apostrophe** is placed **after** the ***s***.
- The **men's racquets** were in the locker.
  men = **possessive case** owning *racquets*.
  men = **plural** but does not end in ***s***, so the apostrophe is placed **before** the ***s***.

3 **Circle** the nouns that are **possessive case** and **insert** the **apostrophe**. **Underline** the noun that is **owned**.

a Rowenas craft work is on the ledge over there.

b The childrens work was on display in the centre.

c Those are the babies rattles on the floor.

d Many of the womens scarves were on sale.

e Did you buy that boys stamp album?

4 **Add** an item **owned** by the word in **bold**.

a The **horses'** ______________________ were on the stand.

b I brushed the **dog's** ______________________.

Answers on page 118

Section test 2C

1 **Circle** the **verb** and **underline** the word that is **nominative case subject** of the **verb**.

- **a** The young boy took the wheelbarrow to the shed.
- **b** Ashley, Carrie and Catie visited the old farm.
- **c** Have you ever been late before?
- **d** Will that swimmer break the record?
- **e** Across the road the wild animals raced.

2 Complete the sentence by **adding** a suitable noun or pronoun that is **nominative case subject** of the **verb**.

- **a** Many strange ______________________ inhabited the region.
- **b** Will ______________________ be leaving for the station?
- **c** The ______________________ believed it to be correct.

3 **Insert** words that are **nominative case complement** of the **verb**.

- **a** Many of the sailors became ___________________.
- **b** She is my best ___________________.
- **c** Are these the ___________________ to use?
- **d** These two children are excellent ___________________.
- **e** Will she be a competent ___________________?

4 **Read** each sentence. Does the sentence have a word that is **objective case governed** by the **verb**? **Circle** the **object**.

- **a** All the animals grazed in the field. Yes ☐ No ☐ *(tick)*
- **b** Did you complete the job on time? Yes ☐ No ☐
- **c** Some of the birds flew across the lake. Yes ☐ No ☐
- **d** Caroline will take it with her. Yes ☐ No ☐
- **e** Have you ever seen the artwork? Yes ☐ No ☐

5 **Read** each sentence. Does the sentence have **two words** that are **objective case governed** by a **preposition**? **Circle** words that are **objective case governed** by a **preposition**. **Underline** the **prepositions**.

- **a** Into the mist the flock of birds vanished. Yes ☐ No ☐ *(tick)*
- **b** Leo took the horses into the stables. Yes ☐ No ☐
- **c** The car turned to the right and then to the left. Yes ☐ No ☐
- **d** My cousin from Melbourne will arrive in the morning. Yes ☐ No ☐
- **e** This foal was born in early August. Yes ☐ No ☐

☞ Answers on page 118

Section test 2C

6 Do these sentences have words that are **objective case governed** by an **infinitive**, **verbal noun** or **participle**? If so, **underline** the **words** in **objective case**.

- **a** Many of them came to buy the fruit. Yes ☐ No ☐ *(tick)*
- **b** Climbing those peaks is a difficult challenge. Yes ☐ No ☐
- **c** The boy riding the mountain bike is my brother. Yes ☐ No ☐

7 **Add** nouns that would be **objective case governed** by the words in **bold**. What **parts** of **speech** are the words in **bold**?

- **a** **To paint** the ______________________ took a long time. (______________)
- **b** The man **wearing** ______________________ came from Brisbane. (______________)
- **c** All the class enjoyed **playing** ______________________. (______________)

8 **Circle** the **nouns** that are **possessive case** and **underline** the **noun** that is **owned**.

- **a** The horses' bridles were on the pegs.
- **b** Has anyone seen Neil's photo album?
- **c** I have taken the officer's rifle.
- **d** Were the girls' dresses set out on the rack?
- **e** Nan's figurines were on display.

9 Add a **noun**, **possessive case**, and an **item** that is **owned**.

- **a** These are ______________________________.
- **b** Were you able to collect ______________________________?
- **c** ______________________ were drenched in the downpour.

10 **Read** each sentence and indicate if the statements are **true** or **false**.

a Over the valley near our town the animals grazed contentedly.

- *animals* = **noun**, **nominative case**, **subject** of the **verb** *grazed*. True ☐ False ☐ *(tick)*
- *valley* = **noun**, **objective case**, **governed** by the **preposition** *over*. True ☐ False ☐
- *contentedly* = **noun**, **objective case**, **governed** by the **verb** *grazed*. True ☐ False ☐

b The adult riding the stallion is a very experienced horsewoman.

- *adult* = **noun**, **nominative case**, **subject** of the **verb** *is*. True ☐ False ☐
- *stallion* = **noun**, **objective case**, **governed** by the **participle** *riding*. True ☐ False ☐
- *horsewoman* = **noun**, **objective case**, **governed** by the **verb** *is*. True ☐ False ☐

c Ned's pets were kept in the shed to avoid the cold weather.

- *shed* = **noun**, **nominative case** of the **verb** *were kept*. True ☐ False ☐
- *weather* = **noun**, **objective case**, **governed** by the **infinitive** *to avoid*. True ☐ False ☐
- *Ned's* = **noun**, **possessive case owning** *pets*. True ☐ False ☐

☞ Answers on page 119

Review test 2

1 **Circle** the **verb**. **Underline** the **subject**.

- **a** Some of the children delivered the booklists.
- **b** All the scientists worked in that building.
- **c** Julia had not completed the work on time.
- **d** These wild animals are running free on the plain.
- **e** The car with a red roof was left in the car park.

2 **Add** a suitable **subject** and **verb** to **complete** these sentences.

- **a** ______________________________ the boxes out.
- **b** ______________________________ the notes for the lesson.
- **c** ______________________________ it.

3 **Circle** the **subject** and **underline** the **predicate**.

- **a** My eldest sister has travelled to New Zealand.
- **b** Which vehicle will you be using?
- **c** Across the rocks the escapee fled quickly.
- **d** By the stream and along the hills the animals wandered.

4 **Circle** the **verbs**. **Underline** the **object**.

- **a** The recruits cleaned these rifles.
- **b** Lina studied her work for several hours.
- **c** Did she sing the song well?
- **d** Was Ken carrying the firewood to the shed?
- **e** Can you tile the kitchen floor for me?

5 **Circle** the **direct objects** and **underline** the **indirect objects**.

- **a** Our friends gave the toy to Brad.
- **b** The shopkeeper showed them the new product.
- **c** Ali gave him a ten dollar note.

6 **Underline** the **complements**. **Circle** the **subject**.

- **a** This vegetable is an eggplant.
- **b** Fleur is a skilful gymnast.
- **c** The view from the window is spectacular.

7 Use *the boy* in the following **situations**.

- **a** as subject: ______________________________
- **b** as object: ______________________________
- **c** as complement: ______________________________

☞ Answers on page 119

Review test 2

8 **Underline** the **first person pronouns** and **circle** the **second person pronouns**.

a We will take you with us.

b I believe that your brother can do better.

c These are ours, but does this one belong to you?

9 **Underline** the **singular** nouns and pronouns and **circle** the **plural** nouns and pronouns.

Last Saturday we had the inter-school sports day. It began early on the oval. The two houses of the school are Torres and Cook. The sprints and jumps were held before lunch. After lunch the relays were held.

10 Correct these sentences by **altering** the **verb**.

a Some boys **is** finishing the work.

____

b A large dish **were** found on the beach.

____

11 **Circle** the **masculine** and **underline** the **feminine** nouns in these sentences.

a The duke went with his sister to the track.

b My brother looked after the ducks in the pen.

c The husband of that woman is riding the black stallion.

12 **Circle** the **common nouns** and **underline** the **neuter nouns**.

a All the cattle and sheep were loaded onto the truck.

b The young children had visited the park regularly.

c Across the road the horses galloped quickly.

13 Use this combination to **create** a **sentence**:

me (first person, singular number), *toys* (third person, plural number)

____

14 **Read** each sentence and **answer** the questions.

a Near the railing next to the shed the jockey waited patiently.

Which word is nominative case subject of the verb *waited*? ____________________

Which word is objective case governed by the preposition *near*? ____________________

Which word is objective case governed by the preposition *to*? ____________________

b The worker's vehicle was damaged in the accident.

Which word is nominative case subject of the verb *was damaged*? ____________________

Which word is possessive case owning *vehicle*? ____________________

Which word is objective case governed by the preposition *in*? ____________________

15 **a** **Use** the word *stealing* as a **participle** so that it **governs** another word in the **objective case**. **Underline** the word it **governs**.

____

b **Use** the word *surfing* as a **verbal noun** so that it **governs** another word in the **objective case**. **Underline** the word it **governs**.

____

Answers on page 119

3 Phrases, sentences and clauses

Phrases – Adjectival

A **phrase** is a group of words **without** a **finite verb**.

An **adjectival phrase describes nouns** or **pronouns** and therefore **does the work** of an **adjective**. These phrases usually **begin** with a **preposition**.

Examples

- The girl **in the red dress** is over here.
  in the red dress = an **adjectival phrase describing** *the girl*
- The vehicle **with a damaged bonnet** was in the yard.
  with a damaged bonnet = an **adjectival phrase describing** *the vehicle*

1 **Underline** the **adjectival phrase** and **circle** the **word** it **describes**.

a It was a huge load of damaged timber.

b My sister with the green hat is down the road.

c Here is the coin of little value.

d Can you collect the book with a blue cover?

e That tree by the fence is in full bloom.

2 **Select** suitable **adjectival phrases** from the box to **describe** the words in **bold**.

with the damaged sails	in a green shirt	in the bag	near the steps
in haste	with an injured leg	with a red roof	

a The kitten ______________________________ was in the shed.

b Have you seen the ships ______________________________?

c Please sweep the path ______________________________.

d The cottage ______________________________ belongs to Sam.

e All the apples ________________________ were bought yesterday.

Single adjectives can often be expressed as **adjectival phrases**.

Example

- Here is the **red haired** boy. (adjective)
- Here is the boy **with red hair**. (adjectival phrase)

3 Draw lines to **match** the **single adjectives** to the **adjectival phrases**.

beautiful	of great depth
mischievous	of great beauty
westerly	with blue eyes
deep	full of mischief
blue-eyed	from the west

4 **Change** the **single adjective** to an **adjectival phrase**.

a The **school** girls sang very well. ______________________________

b The **jungle** track was difficult to follow. ______________________________

☞ Answers on page 119

Phrases – Adverbial

A **phrase** is a group of words **without** a **finite verb**.

An **adverbial phrase** describes a **verb**. It **does the work** of an **adverb**.

Adverbial phrases usually **begin** with a **preposition**.

Examples

- He <u>rode</u> along **with great care**. (adverbial phrase of **manner** tells how he *rode*)
- She <u>went</u> there **in the morning**. (adverbial phrase of **time** tells when she *went*)
- <u>Do</u> not <u>leave</u> it **at the gate**. (adverbial phrase of **place** tells where it is *not to be left*)
- **Because of the storm** the race <u>was cancelled</u>. (adverbial phrase of *reason* tells why it *was cancelled*)

1 **Underline** the **adverbial phrases** and **circle** the **verb** they **describe**.

a The children went into the village.

b By seven o'clock all the animals were quiet.

c They left early for no reason.

d The briefcase was left on the train.

e Will you collect the vase after the meeting?

2 **Select** suitable **adverbial phrases** from the box to **describe** the words in **bold**.

after the meeting	in the long grass	on the road
at once	to the celebrations	for their protection

a The box **was hidden** ____________________.

b Many of them **came** ____________________.

c ____________________ the officer **left** the building.

d Some of the creatures **had been locked** away ____________________.

e **Do** your work ____________________.

3 **Underline** the **adverbial phrases**. **Indicate** whether they tell us **how**, **when**, **where** or **why**.

a For some time the girls waited at the dock. __________

b Several of them played in that place. __________

c My cousin went to the meeting because of problems. __________

d All of the horses galloped in a steady manner. __________

e Samantha saw the ducks swim across the pond. __________

Quick check

Underline the **adverbial phrases** and **circle** the **words** they **describe**.

During the day the students played in the paddock. Because of the windy conditions they flew their kites above the treeline. Some well prepared kites could be seen from several kilometres away. At dusk they left the paddock.

Answers on page 119

Phrases – Verbal noun

A **phrase** is a group of words **without a finite verb**.

A **verbal noun phrase does the work** of a **noun**. It **begins** with a **verbal noun**. It can be used in different ways in sentences.

Example

- **Flying kites** is great fun. (verbal noun phrase as **subject** of the sentence)
- They all enjoy **flying kites**. (verbal noun phrase as **object** of the sentence)
- His great pastime is **flying kites**. (verbal noun phrase as **complement** of the sentence)
- He is fond of **flying kites**. (verbal noun phrase as **object** of the preposition *of*)

1 **Underline** the **verbal noun phrases** in these sentences.

a Buying the car took a long time.

b Extending the boundary fence was hard work.

c The athlete enjoyed running the marathon.

d Practising the piano became important to the girl.

e Many of them were capable of fixing the machine.

2 **Use** these **phrases introduced** by **verbal nouns** in sentences.

a jumping the hurdles: ______________________________

b catching butterflies: ______________________________

3 **Underline** the **verbal noun phrases** in these sentences. **Indicate** whether the phrase is acting as a **subject**, **object** or **complement**.

a All of them enjoyed building the model. ______________

b Selecting the prizes caused her to be late. ______________

c His favourite activity was riding in the parade. ______________

d Wandering the highway was not his idea of fun. ______________

4 **Use** this **phrase** as the **complement** in a simple sentence.

watching television: ______________________________

5 **Select** suitable **verbal noun phrases** from the box to **complete** these sentences.

riding his trail bike	creating interesting artwork	minding the machinery
working quietly	at the corner	completing crossword puzzles

a The young boy enjoys ______________________________.

b My young sister is good at ______________________________.

c ______________________________ is Henry's greatest skill.

Quick check

Underline the **verbal noun phrases**. **Circle** the **verbal noun**.

1 She was not capable of lifting the parcel.

2 Joining the army is his ambition.

3 Emily likes singing popular songs.

Answers on pages 119–120

Phrases – Participle and infinitive

A **phrase** is a group of words **without** a **finite verb**.

Participle phrases

A **participle phrase does the work** of an **adjective**. It **begins** with a **past** or **present participle**.

Examples

- The shed **struck by the tree** was damaged badly.
  The **participle phrase** is *struck by the tree*. The **participle beginning** the **phrase** is *struck*.
  The phrase points out **which** shed, so its function is **adjectival**.
- The girls **practising goal shooting** are new to the school.
  The **participle phrase** is *practising goal shooting*.
  The phrase points out **which** girls, so its function is **adjectival**.

1 **Underline** the **participle phrases** in these sentences. **Circle** the **participle**.

- **a** The animal injured in the accident was taken to the vet.
- **b** The girl running towards us is Sally.
- **c** All of the books carried by the student were brand new.

2 **Select** a **participle phrase** from the box to **complete** these sentences.

practised by the men	damaged in the fire	broken away
running towards the cliff	found in the shipwreck	

- **a** The coins ______________________________ were very old.
- **b** The machine ________________________ was no longer of any use.
- **c** The mast ________________________ by the wind fell into the sea.

Infinitive phrases

An **infinitive phrase begins** with an **infinitive** and can be used in different ways in sentences.

Examples

- They came **to polish the car**. (infinitive phrase telling why—acts as an **adverb**)
- The horses **to ride in the event** are here. (infinitive phrase telling which horses—acts as an **adjective**)
- **To win the prize** was his intention. (infinitive phrase used as **subject**)
- They wanted **to win the prize**. (infinitive phrase used as **object**)
- His main aim was **to win the prize**. (infinitive phrase used as **complement**)

3 **Underline** the **infinitive phrases**.

- **a** All had arrived to celebrate her birthday.
- **b** The players to compete in the game are here.

4 **Underline** the **infinitive phrase** and **indicate** whether it is being used as **subject**, **object** or **complement**.

- **a** To view the statue was his greatest wish. ______________
- **b** She needed to view the statue. ______________
- **c** Their intention was to view the statue. ______________

☞ Answers on page 120

Section test 3A

1 **Underline** the **adjectival phrases** and **circle** the **words** that they **describe**.

a Here is the coat of many colours.

b His brother in the red shirt is eight years old.

c That is the bracelet with the valuable emeralds.

d Will you deliver the book with a green cover?

2 **Select** suitable **adjectival phrases** from the box to **describe** the words in **bold**.

of blue crystal	with the blue sails	on the small stage
in the new home	with a yellow garage door	

a The **yacht** ______________________ belongs to our neighbour.

b Have you seen the **house** ______________________?

c The **vase** ______________________ contained many blooms.

3 **Change** the **single adjective** to an **adjectival phrase**.

a The **southerly** wind blew strongly. ______________________

____

b The **blue-eyed** girl was a fine athlete. ______________________

____

4 **Underline** the **adverbial phrases** and **circle** the **verbs** they **describe**.

a During the morning they went to the Spring Fair.

b The workers had completed the job by five o'clock.

c The box was left beside the road.

d Can you leave the grounds after the display?

5 **Select** suitable **adverbial phrases** to **describe** the words in **bold**.

with a red cover	at the far gate	during the long evening
of several colours	on account of illness	of great strength

a All the riders were waiting ______________________.

b ______________________ the machines rattled by.

c She was absent ______________________.

6 **Change** the single adverb **to an adverbial phrase**.

a They lived **comfortably** in the new house. ______________________

____

b The work was done **carefully**. ______________________

7 **Read** the sentence and **answer** the questions.

Near the house with the red roof is a barn in poor condition.

Which **phrase** describes the noun *house*? ______________________

Which **phrase** describes the noun *barn*? ______________________

What is the **adverbial phrase**? ______________________

Answers on page 120

Section test 3A

8 **Underline** the **verbal noun phrases** in these sentences.

- **a** Studying the subject took a great deal of time.
- **b** All of them enjoyed riding trail bikes.
- **c** The most important thing to her was completing her artwork.
- **d** She was incapable of mending the torn jacket.

9 **Identify** the **verbal noun phrase** as **subject**, **object**, **complement** or **object** of a preposition.

- **a** Running a marathon was his ambition. ____________________
- **b** They were all fond of playing netball. ____________________
- **c** Ivan's greatest love was singing on stage. ____________________
- **d** Matt disliked practising the piano. ____________________

10 **Use** these **phrases** in **sentences** introduced by **verbal nouns**.

- **a** collecting the shells: ____

  ____
- **b** lifting the heavy weight: ____

  ____

11 **Underline** the **participle phrases** in these sentences. **Circle** the **participle**.

- **a** The tree blown by the strong wind finally crashed to the ground.
- **b** The boy walking quickly is going to the game.
- **c** All of the charts completed correctly were displayed.

12 **Use** these phrases as **participle phrases** in **sentences**.

- **a** gleaming brightly: ____

  ____
- **b** washed carefully: ____

  ____

13 **Underline** the **infinitive phrases**.

- **a** They arrived early to plant the seed.
- **b** It was difficult to complete the assignment.
- **c** They went there to repair the engine.

14 **Identify** the **infinitive phrases** as having the **function** of **adverb**, **adjective**, **subject**, **object** or **complement**.

- **a** Many of them came to finish the work. ____________________
- **b** To paint the fence took many days. ____________________
- **c** Sharon really wanted to win the prize. ____________________
- **d** The cars to be test driven were in the car yard. ____________________
- **e** His future goal was to manage the factory. ____________________

15 Use *to make the bed* as an **infinitive phrase acting** as an **adverb**.

____

☞ Answers on page 120

Simple sentences – Statements, commands, requests

A **simple sentence** contains a **finite verb** and consists of **one main clause**. A finite verb has a **subject**.

A simple sentence contains a **subject** and **predicate**.

- The **subject** is the **naming part** of a sentence.
- The **predicate** is the **telling part** of a sentence.

Examples

<u>My brother Ken</u> (subject—names the person)	<u>walked to the gate early</u>. (predicate—tells us what the person does)
<u>The boy</u> (subject)	<u>collected the parcels</u>. (predicate)
<u>Sharon</u> (subject)	<u>enjoys watching films</u>. (predicate)
<u>Colin</u> (subject)	<u>became a navy pilot</u>. (predicate)
<u>All the people</u> (subject)	<u>went into town</u>. (predicate)

Statements

A **statement** is a **simple sentence** that **states** a **fact**, **opinion** or **possibility**.

Examples

- This artist has completed many works. (fact)
- All of them may visit the museum. (possibility)
- This is a very poor road surface. (opinion)

1 **Identify** these sentences as stating a **fact**, **opinion** or **possibility**.

- **a** Marcus has driven there many times. ____________________
- **b** Your homework has been done well. ____________________
- **c** Kelly might win the event. ____________________
- **d** The young lad can swim the river. ____________________

2 **Circle** the **subjects** and **underline** the **predicates**.

- **a** Many of them changed the markings.
- **b** Anita and Kevin watered the garden this morning.
- **c** These books belong to Jonathon.

Commands and requests

A **command** or **request** is a simple sentence that **requires** an **action** or **response**. In these sentences, the **subject is not stated**. The subject is really *you* (either **singular** or **plural number**) and is said to be **understood**.

Examples

- **Stop** that noise. (*stop* = the verb)
- Please **collect** all the papers. (*collect* = the verb)
- **Take** these at once. (*take* = the verb)

3 Are these sentences **commands** or **requests**? **Tick** the correct box and **underline** the **verb**.

- **a** Follow that car. Yes ☐ No ☐
- **b** Why are you here? Yes ☐ No ☐
- **c** Clean your plate well. Yes ☐ No ☐
- **d** Finish that work please. Yes ☐ No ☐

☞ Answers on page 120

Simple sentences – Interrogative and exclamatory

A **simple sentence** is one that contains a **finite verb** and consists of **one main clause**.

Interrogative sentences

An **interrogative sentence** asks a **question**. A question requires a **spoken** or **written answer**.

Examples

- Will you collect the parcel?
- Where did Paul go?
- Does his brother work here?

1 **Circle** the **verbs** and **underline** the **subjects** in these **interrogative sentences**.

- **a** Can the children deliver the bread?
- **b** Why are you in this out-of-bounds area?
- **c** Can the horse jump the fence?
- **d** When did Hank find that old coin?
- **e** Are these apples ripe and juicy?

An **interrogative sentence** can be **turned into** a **statement** by **changing** the **order** of the **words**.

Example

- Did Sam repair the machine? (interrogative)
- Sam did repair the machine. (statement)

2 **Change** these **interrogative sentences** into **statements**.

- **a** May I complete the map next week?

  ____

- **b** Has she begun that part of the artwork?

  ____

- **c** Will Peter and Michael look after the animal?

  ____

Exclamatory sentences

An **exclamatory sentence** is a **simple sentence** that **shows strong feeling**. It has an **exclamation mark (!)** at the end.

Often there is **no verb, subject or object** included. In these cases the verb, subject or object is **understood**.

Examples

- How cold it was!
- What a terrible mistake he made!
- What a catch! (Subject *it* and verb *was* are **understood**.)

3 Are the following sentences **exclamatory**? **Tick** Yes or No. If yes, **write** the **words understood**.

- **a** Where is he? Yes ☐ No ☐ ______________
- **b** How terrible! Yes ☐ No ☐ ______________
- **c** What luck! Yes ☐ No ☐ ______________

☞ Answers on page 120

Compound sentences

A **compound sentence** is made up of **two** or **more** parts called **clauses**.
These clauses are **joined** by conjunctions *and*, *but* and *or*.

Examples

- They came to the spot (principal clause) and they began to unload the boat. (principal clause)
- He collected the pots (principal clause) but could not carry them to the car. (principal clause)

These sentences could have been written as **two simple sentences**:

- They came to the spot. They began to unload the boat.
- He collected the pots. He could not carry them to the car.

1 **Underline** the **two principal clauses** in these sentences. **Circle** the **conjunctions**.

a The man took the car and collected the parcels.

b He went to the beach but he did not have a swim.

c She will go to the show or she will stay at home.

2 **Use** the **conjunctions** *and*, *but* and *or* to **join** these pairs of sentences.

a The children will leave for the beach. They will take their swimming gear with them.

____

____

b Many of them stayed at the zoo. They did not find the lost purse.

____

____

c The young animal will cross the river. It may remain in this spot.

____

____

3 **Underline** the **conjunctions** and **circle** the **verbs** in the **two principal clauses**.

a Tom went to the park and played on the swings.

b The young girl collected the money but did not spend it.

c Philippa will be travelling to Queensland and will be staying in Cairns.

d They will open the presents or leave them until later.

4 **Read** the sentences and answer **true** or **false**.

a She wanted the coat but did not have enough money.

but = the **conjunction** True ☐ False ☐ *(tick)*

The **subject** of the **first principal clause** = *she* True ☐ False ☐

The **verb** in the **second principal clause** = *did not have* True ☐ False ☐

b The animals will be moved to the yards or will remain in the paddock.

There are **two principal clauses**. True ☐ False ☐

The **conjunction** = *and* True ☐ False ☐

The **subject** of the **first principal clause** = *yards* True ☐ False ☐

Answers on page 120

Complex sentences

A **complex sentence** is made up of **two** or **more clauses**. One of the clauses is the **principal clause** and the others are called **subordinate clauses**.

Subordinate clauses can do the work of **adjectives**, **adverbs** or **nouns**.

Examples

- There is the house (principal clause) — **that** I own. (subordinate clause working as **adjective**)
- He did not leave (principal clause) — **until** it was late. (subordinate clause working as **adverb**)
- I do not know (principal clause) — **when** it will be read. (subordinate clause working as **noun**)

1 **Underline** the **principal clause** and **circle** the **joining word**.

a There is the building that is in need of repair.

b She was the only person who did not enjoy the play.

c They will leave before us if they are ready.

d The gang toiled that they might finish on time.

2 **Select** a suitable **subordinate clause** from the box to **complete** these **complex sentences**.

it had been a good contest	was brand new	is either of her sisters
did you enjoy	the game will be completed	was held last week

a We travelled in the car which ____________________.

b I do not know when ____________________.

c She played in the contest that ____________________.

d Karen is taller than ____________________.

3 **Select** suitable **principal clauses** from the box to **complete** the **complex sentences**.

It took them to the city	Here are the books	It will be read
He did not enjoy the play	They played out in the yard	She attended the concert

a ____________________ that were on the floor.

b ____________________ although she was sick.

c ____________________ until it was dark.

4 Read this sentence. Answer **true** or **false**.

The girl drove the car that had a red roof until she saw the sign near the driveway.

There are **three clauses**. True ❑ False ❑ *(tick)*

The girl drove the car = the **principal clause**. True ❑ False ❑

The joining words = *that* and *until* True ❑ False ❑

5 **Write** a **complex sentence** with **three clauses** using these **two joining words**: *who* and *when*.

____

____

Answers on page 121

Compound-complex sentences

A **compound-complex sentence** is made up of **three** or **more clauses**. It contains **two** or **more principal clauses** and **one** or **more subordinate clauses**. The **subordinate clauses** can **do the work** of **adjectives**, **adverbs** or **nouns**.

Examples

- Fiona visited the show (principal clause) and bought the boat (principal clause) that was on display. (subordinate clause)
- When they reached the city (subordinate clause) where the treasure was kept (subordinate clause) the gang of thieves hired a car (principal clause) and began planning the robbery. (principal clause)

1 Are these **compound-complex sentences**? **Circle** the **subordinate clauses** and **underline** the **principal clauses**.

a After the party was over all the relatives boarded the train which was to leave at eight o'clock. Yes ☐ No ☐ *(tick)*

b If you see the vehicle that has a red roof please advise the police department and officers will follow it. Yes ☐ No ☐

c We will complete the task and move on to the next one when we are advised that it is time to do so. Yes ☐ No ☐

2 **Select** a suitable **principal clause** from the box to **complete** these **compound-complex sentences**.

there is snow on the mountains	it is a long way	He will go to the museum
it could not be found	She will enjoy the cakes	he is in the way

a I know the way to the shop but ______________________ and I am not sure if the shop actually stocks those items.

b ______________________ or he will go to the zoo which is down the road that leads to Earlville.

3 **Select two clauses** from the box to **complete** this **compound-complex sentence**.

they were not sure	they enjoyed it very much
was held in the concert hall	that goes through the town

Sue and her brother went to the concert which ______________________

______________________ and ______________________

______________________.

4 **Read** this sentence and **identify** the clauses as **principal** or **subordinate**.

Sharon visited the village ______________

where the lavender was grown ______________

and she bought several bottles of oil ______________

which were very cheap. ______________

Answers on page 121

Section test 3B

1 **Identify** the **simple sentences** as **statements**, **commands**, **requests, interrogative** or **exclamatory sentences**.

a He caught it. ________________

b Stop the car at once. ________________

c The huge lion roared loudly. ________________

d Will you finish the work? ________________

e She did pick the flowers this morning. ________________

f How hot it is! ________________

g Who collected the first prize? ________________

h Let it go. ________________

2 **Change** the **interrogative sentences** into **statements**.

a Has Michelle been to the markets?

____

b Are the boys sailing across the bay now?

____

c Can the printer have the work ready by one o'clock?

____

3 **Write sentences** according to these **instructions**.

a An interrogative sentence beginning with *where*:

____

b An exclamatory sentence beginning with *how*:

____

c A command or request beginning with *hold*:

____

d A statement beginning with *the animal*:

____

4 **Circle** the **subjects** and **underline** the **predicates**.

a Many of the ships were anchored in the channel.

b Stop it here please.

c Start the car immediately.

d Those relatives visited him early yesterday.

5 **Read** each sentence and answer **true** or **false**.

a Take it to the desk over there.

This is an **interrogative sentence**. True ☐ False ☐ *(tick)*

The **verb** is *take*. True ☐ False ☐

The **subject** *you* is **understood**. True ☐ False ☐

☞ Answers on page 121

b What a throw!

This is an **exclamatory sentence**. True ☐ False ☐ *(tick)*

The **subject** and **verb** are **understood**. True ☐ False ☐

A **suitable subject** and **verb** could be *it was*. True ☐ False ☐

6 **Underline** the **conjunctions** in these sentences.

a They will carry the parcels or have them taken by truck.

b Bronwen could not arrange the flowers or pack them carefully.

c Many of them went to Granville and left the next day.

7 Use one of the **conjunctions** in **question 6** to **combine** these **two sentences** into a **compound sentence**.

All the people collected the money. None of it was misplaced.

____

____

8 **Read** the sentence and **answer** the questions.

The musicians played at the town hall but did not leave until late.

Is *but* a conjunction? Yes ☐ No ☐ *(tick)*

Is the **subject** of the **first principal clause** *musicians*? Yes ☐ No ☐

Is the **verb** in the **second principal clause** *did until*? Yes ☐ No ☐

9 **Circle** the **joining words** and **underline** the **subordinate clauses**.

a She drove the vehicle that had been used last week.

b There is the bus which has travelled to town.

c Judy is much taller than her brother is.

10 **Read** the sentence and **answer** the questions.

The boy visited the library which was on the corner so that he could borrow the new novel.

a Are there **three clauses**? Yes ☐ No ☐ *(tick)*

b What is the **principal clause**? ____________________

c What are the **joining words**? ____________________

11 **Read** these sentences and **answer** the questions.

a If the bus is late, we will go by train which leaves at three o'clock tomorrow.

What is the **principal clause**? ____________________

What is the **first subordinate clause**? ____________________

What is the **second subordinate clause**? ____________________

b When you collect the parcel that was forwarded to you, take it to the shop and have it signed for.

This is a **compound-complex sentence**. Yes ☐ No ☐ *(tick)*

There are **two principal clauses**. Yes ☐ No ☐

There are **two subordinate clauses**. Yes ☐ No ☐

What are the **joining words**? ____________________

Answers on page 121

Clauses – Adjectival clauses and relative pronouns

An **adjectival clause** describes a **noun** or **pronoun** in one of the other clauses in a sentence.

Adjectival clauses begin with a **relative pronoun**: *who*, *whom*, *whose*, *which*, *that*.

Example

- Mukesh saw the boy (principal clause) who lives down the street. (adjectival clause)
- There is the book (principal clause) which I recently read. (adjectival clause)

1 **Underline** the **adjectival clause** and **circle** the **relative pronouns**.

a This is the cat that I own.

b Here is the animal which ran away.

c I saw the girl whom you knew.

d There is the girl whose father is sick.

Who, *whom* and *whose* are used for **people**; *that* and *which* are used for **animals** and **nouns** of **neuter gender**.

2 **Combine** these pairs of sentences into a **single sentence** with a **principal clause** and an **adjectival clause**.

a John saw the girls. They completed the work. ____________________

b Here are the animals. I saw them. ____________________

c This is the fence. He took it away. ____________________

3 **Separate** these **complex sentences** into **two simple sentences**.

a She found the road that led to the old hut. ____________________

b The box that belongs to John is here. ____________________

c The woman whose husband is away is very ill. ____________________

4 **Select** suitable **adjectival clauses** from the box to **complete** these sentences.

was on the lake	broke his leg in the accident	was caught in the jungle trap
lives in the stable	looked quietly at the animals	

a The boy **who** ____________________ is my brother.

b The animal **that** ____________________ was injured.

c My sailing boat **which** ____________________ was lost.

Quick check

Underline the **adjectival clauses**.

1 Sue watched the house which had a green roof.

2 This is the child whose father is overseas.

Answers on page 121

Clauses – Adjectival clauses, relative pronouns and antecedents

An **adjectival clause** describes a **noun or pronoun** in one of the other clauses in a sentence.

Adjectival clauses begin with a **relative pronoun**: *who*, *whom*, *whose*, *which*, *that*.

The word the clause **describes** is called the **antecedent**.

Example

- There is the stapler (principal clause) which I own. (adjectival clause)

  which is the **relative pronoun** and *stapler* is the **antecedent** (the word in the principal clause that the adjectival clause describes).

1 **Underline** the **adjectival clauses**. **Circle** the **relative pronouns** and the **antecedents**.

a There is the case which belonged to Jessica.

b Do you know the way to reach the station that the Ellis family owns?

c He passed the ball to Sam who scored the winning goal.

d The old sailor couldn't remember the young child who met him at the dock.

Sometimes the **adjectival clause** is **between** the **first** and **second parts** of the **principal clause**.

Example

- The car (first part of principal clause) which I own (adjectival clause) was bought in Sydney. (second part of principal clause)

2 **Underline** the first and second parts of the **principal clauses**. **Circle** the **relative pronouns** and **antecedents**.

a The boy whom I saw there was a stranger.

b The strange weapon that was found in the forest will be handed in.

c The competition which was arranged yesterday was very interesting.

3 **Join** these pairs of sentences to form **complex sentences**. **Underline** the **relative pronoun** and **circle** the **antecedent**.

a The car is here. It was found near the station.

____

b Our friend is new to the district. He came here from the country.

____

____

c I have a small cardboard box. All my letters are kept in it.

____

____

4 **a** **Use** *who sat here* as an **adjectival clause**.

____

b **Use** *that had been damaged* as an **adjectival clause**.

____

☞ Answers on page 121

Clauses – Adjectival clauses with relative pronoun omitted

An **adjectival clause** describes a **noun** or **pronoun** in one of the **other clauses** in a **sentence**.

Adjectival clauses begin with a **relative pronoun**: *who*, *whom*, *whose*, *which*, *that*.

Sometimes the **relative pronoun** is **omitted**.

Example

- This is the box (principal clause) I want. (adjectival clause)
  The relative pronoun (*that* or *which*) has been left out.

1 **Underline** the **principal clause**. **Place** a ✓ where the relative pronoun is left out. **Write** the **relative pronoun**.

a Many of the children we saw were very happy. ________

b Are these the pencils you want? ________

c Stephanie bought the car Max sold. ________

d In the box he put in the car were some old clothes. ________

2 **Complete** these sentences using **adjectival clauses with the relative pronoun omitted**. **Write** the **relative pronoun** at the end of the sentence.

a She made ________ (________)

b Malcolm collected ________

________ (________)

3 **Combine** these sentences into a **complex sentence** with the **relative pronoun omitted**.

a There is the new car. I drove it away. ________

b Maria found the purse. You lost it at the show.

____

Sometimes when writing **complex sentences** using an **adjectival clause**, a **preposition is needed before** the **relative pronoun**.

Example

- Two simple sentences: I saw the rock. The lighthouse stands on it.
- One complex sentence: I saw the rock (principal clause) **on** which the lighthouse stands. (adjectival clause)

4 **Underline** the **adjectival clause**. **Circle** the **preposition** that comes **before** the **relative pronoun**.

a Here is the pool into which the tyres were thrown.

b The girl of whom I spoke is absent today.

c These chairs on which the visitors sat need to be returned.

5 **Combine** these sentences into a **complex sentence**. **Circle** the **preposition before** the **relative pronoun**.

The road went past the farm. We walked along it. ________

____

Answers on page 122

Clauses – Adverbial clauses of manner, time, place and reason

Adverbial clauses do the work of an **adverb**. They can tell **how**, **when**, **where** or **why** an action takes place. They begin with a **conjunction**.

Examples

- The boys worked (principal clause) as they had always done. (adverbial clause telling **how**—manner)
- Richard and Rob left (principal clause) when the sun went down. (adverbial clause telling **when**—time)
- She will wait (principal clause) where she has been told. (adverbial clause telling **where**—place)
- Ben was late (principal clause) because he was sick. (adverbial clause telling **why**—reason)

1 **Underline** the **adverbial clause**. **Circle** the **word** that **begins** it.

a The young boy did as he was told.

b The children awoke before the sun appeared.

c As I was leaving the park I saw the animal.

d The animals are grazing where the grass is green.

e We came home for we could see a storm on the horizon.

2 **Add** an **adverbial clause** beginning with the words in **bold**. **Write** the **type** of **adverbial clause** in the brackets.

a All of them played **as if** ____________________. (________)

b Felicity and Helen waited **until** ____________________. (________)

c They will go **where** ____________________. (________)

d The job could not be done **because** ____________________. (________)

3 **Use** these **adverbial clauses** in **complex sentences**.

a Whenever the wind blew strongly ____________________

____

b Lest we should lose the way ____________________

____

An **adverbial phrase** (which does not contain a finite verb) **can be expanded** into a **clause** by adding a **finite verb**.

Example

- Adverbial phrase: On sighting the animal we fled.
- Adverbial clause: When we sighted the animal we fled.

4 **Change** the **adverbial phrases** into **adverbial clauses**. **Use** the **conjunctions** shown in brackets.

a Finish the work **before my departure**. (before)

____________________.

b The entertainers put on one show **at sunset**. (when)

____________________.

Answers on page 122

Clauses – Adverbial clauses of condition, comparison, concession, result and purpose

Adverbial clauses do the work of an **adverb**.

They can also show:

- the **condition** under which something is done
- a **comparison** between things
- a **concession** or the granting of something
- the **result** of some action
- the **purpose** for which some action was done.

Examples

- We will succeed <u>if we work hard</u>. (Working hard is a **condition** of success.)
- She is taller <u>than her brother is</u>. (The girl and her brother are being **compared**.)
- The boy worked hard <u>though he was ill</u>. (**Conceding** or allowing for his illness, the boy still worked hard.)
- He ran so quickly <u>that he outdistanced them all</u>. (The **result** of his fast pace was that he outdistanced them.)
- They worked hard <u>so that they could leave early</u>. (The **purpose** of their hard work was so that they could leave early.)

1 **Underline** the **adverbial clause** and **circle** the word that begins it.

- **a** Unless the wind changes we cannot leave.
- **b** Angie is much taller than her aunt is.
- **c** He bought the article although it was expensive.
- **d** The animal struggled so that it might escape.
- **e** She did not finish it although she tried hard.

2 **Add adverbial clauses** beginning with the words in **bold**.

- **a** They went **although** ____________________.
- **b** This crate is much heavier **than** ____________________.
- **c** All the children will go **if** ____________________.
- **d** The team stayed behind **so that** ____________________.

3 **Use** the following as adverbial clauses in **complex sentences**.

- **a** (that he might escape) ____________________

  ____________________.
- **b** (although the mine was abandoned) ____________________

  ____________________.

4 **Change** the **adverbial phrases** into **adverbial clauses**. **Use** the **conjunction** shown in brackets.

- **a** **Though feeling sick** he continued the race. (though)

  ____________________.
- **b** She will go to the circus **if possible**. (if)

  ____________________.

Answers on page 122

Adjectival and adverbial clauses

How much do you know?

1 **Underline** the **adjectival clauses** and **circle** the **relative pronouns**. Checkpoint page 64

- **a** There is the toy which Sam bought.
- **b** Jan spoke to the girl whom you met.
- **c** Scott collected the parcel that was left on the step.

2 **Combine** this pair of **simple sentences** into a **complex sentence** and **underline** the **relative pronoun**.

I saw the painting. Fiona had completed it.

____

3 **Underline** the **adjectival clause**. **Circle** the **relative pronoun** and the **antecedent**. Checkpoint page 65

- **a** Can you follow the path that leads to the well?
- **b** She gave the prize to Ellen who had come first.
- **c** Our friends, who came from Gosford, arrived yesterday.

4 **Combine** these pairs of sentences into a **complex sentence** with the **relative pronoun omitted**. **Write** the **relative pronoun** at the **end** of the **sentence**. Checkpoint page 66

- **a** There is the new boat. Rosetta bought it.

  ____ (__________)

- **b** Hugo had collected the prize. He thoroughly deserved it.

  ____ (__________)

5 **Read** the sentence and answer **true** or **false**. Checkpoint pages 67–68

a They waited at the house until the storm was over.

There are **two clauses**.	True ☐	False ☐	*(tick)*
The **conjunction** joining the **clauses** is *until*.	True ☐	False ☐	
until the storm was over is an **adjectival clause**.	True ☐	False ☐	
until the storm was over is an **adverbial clause**.	True ☐	False ☐	

b The building could not be completed because the rain fell heavily.

There are **two clauses**.	True ☐	False ☐	*(tick)*
The **subordinate clause** is an **adverbial clause**.	True ☐	False ☐	
It is an **adverbial clause** telling us **why**.	True ☐	False ☐	
The verb in the **adverbial clause** is *completed*.	True ☐	False ☐	

6 **Add** an **adverbial clause** beginning with the word in **bold**.

- **a** **Though** ______________________________ he joined the club.
- **b** This product is more expensive **than** __________________________.

7 **Change** the **adverbial phrase** into an **adverbial clause**. **Use** the **conjunction** shown in brackets.

They collected the tools to finish the work. (*so that*)

____

Answers on page 122

Clauses – Noun clauses (subject, object, complement)

A **noun clause** begins with a **conjunction**. It can be the **subject**, **object** or **complement** of a **verb** in **another clause**.

Examples

- What she is completing (noun clause subject of *takes*) takes special skills. (principal clause)
- The teacher said (principal clause) that I should finish it. (noun clause object of *said*)
- The reason for his absence was (principal clause) that he was ill. (noun clause complement of *was*)

1 **Underline** the **noun clauses** in these sentences and **circle** the **conjunctions**.

a What he has done I do not know.

b She had forgotten that the cat was in the house.

c His excuse was that the paper had been lost.

d When the house will be painted has not been worked out.

2 **Underline** the **noun clauses** and indicate whether they are acting as **subject**, **object** or **complement**.

a That we had taken the wrong turn became evident. ________

b Jack saw that the car was brand new. ________

c Whether the gold will be found is not clear. ________

d The students believed that it was a new book. ________

e His order was that they storm the barricades. ________

3 **Add** suitable **noun clauses** acting as **subject**, **object** or **complement**.

a (subject) What ____ is written here.

b (object) The people believed that ____.

c (complement) My thoughts are that ____.

Sometimes the **conjunction** can be **left out**, especially if the **noun clause** is **acting** as an **object**.

Example

- She said we cannot go. ➠ She said (principal clause) (that) we cannot go. (noun clause)

4 **Mark** with a ✔ where the conjunctions are omitted. **Underline** the **noun clauses**.

a All of the tourists told us it was not safe.

b I am sure you will succeed.

c Many of the team members said he would be able to join them.

Answers on page 122

Clauses – Noun clauses (object of participle, preposition or verbal noun, in apposition)

A **noun clause** begins with a **conjunction**.

Object of participle, preposition or verbal noun

A noun clause can be the **object** of a **participle**, **preposition** or **verbal noun**.

Examples

- Annoyed by (part of principal clause) **what had been said,** (noun clause object of preposition *by*) they walked away. (rest of principal clause)
- He was keen on finding (principal clause) **what had been completed**. (noun clause object of verbal noun *finding*)
- Fearing (part of principal clause) **that he would be late,** (noun clause object of participle *fearing*) my cousin hurried along. (rest of principal clause)

1 **Underline** the **noun clauses** and **circle** the **conjunctions**.

a Confused by what he had been told the soldier waited.

b Saskia was amused by discovering where the kitten had hidden.

c Understanding what had happened was important to him.

2 **Underline** the **noun clauses** and **indicate** whether they are **acting** as **object** of a **preposition**, **verbal noun** or **participle**.

a The miners were delighted on locating where the diamonds were. ____________

b Scared by what they had seen they galloped away. ____________

c The students realising that there was danger escaped easily. ____________

d Angered by what had been done the workers left the job. ____________

3 **Write** a **sentence** using *what had been left behind* as a noun clause in two different ways.

a **object** of a **preposition**: ____________

____

b **object** of a **verbal noun**: ____________

____

In apposition

A noun clause can also be used to **make clear exactly what a writer means**. It is said to be in **apposition** and is placed **next to** or **close to** the **word** it is **explaining**. The word *apposition* means *adds to*.

Example

- A report (part of principal clause) **that the helicopter had crashed** (noun clause in apposition with *report*) was on the news. (rest of principal clause)

In this case, the **noun clause provides** more **information** about the report.

4 **Underline** the **noun clauses** and **circle** the words they **describe**.

a The fact that he had won the race was well known.

b This rumour that he had been to the village before was circulated widely.

c Those glad tidings that spread around the town caused great joy.

Answers on pages 122–123

Noun clauses

1 **Underline** the **subordinate clause** in these sentences. **Tick** the boxes if they are **noun clauses**.

- **a** What he said to me could not be believed. ☐
- **b** She went to the fair after she had completed the work. ☐
- **c** The reason was that it had been left outside. ☐
- **d** She did not remember that the cat was in the box. ☐
- **e** Dean had taken the dog that had been injured. ☐

2 **Underline** the **noun clause**. Indicate whether it is acting as a **subject**, **object** or **complement**.

- **a** That the car was not damaged at all was almost a miracle. ____________
- **b** It is still not clear why the boy ran home. ____________
- **c** Her instructions were that she should bring the parcels. ____________

3 **Mark** with a ✓ where the conjunctions are omitted. **Underline** the **noun clauses**.

- **a** All the children said it was a great event.
- **b** Sharon was sure she would succeed.
- **c** They were all told it was a dangerous climb.

4 Use *that it had been damaged* in sentences the **way shown**.

- **a** noun clause **subject**: ____

  ____
- **b** noun clause **object**: ____

  ____

5 **Underline** the **noun clauses** and indicate whether they are acting as object of a **preposition**, **verbal noun** or **participle**.

- **a** Knowing how it worked was very important. ____________
- **b** George, understanding that it was urgent, began at once. ____________
- **c** Sarah, puzzled by what she had seen, began to run away. ____________

6 **Read** the sentences and **answer** the questions.

- **a** Fascinated by what he had seen, he began photographing the magnificent view.

  what he had seen is a **noun clause object** of the **preposition** *by*. Yes ☐ No ☐ *(tick)*

  The **conjunction** is *what*. Yes ☐ No ☐

  The verb in the **principal clause** is *photographing*. Yes ☐ No ☐
- **b** The information, that the criminal had been active in the area some time ago, was relayed to the police.

  The information was relayed to the police is the principal clause. Yes ☐ No ☐

  that the criminal had been active in the area some time ago is a **noun clause** in **apposition** with *information*. Yes ☐ No ☐

☞ Answers on page 123

Section test 3C

1 **Underline** the **adjectival clauses** and **circle** the **relative pronouns**.

- **a** There is the animal that was treated by the vet.
- **b** Did you see the woman whom I met?
- **c** The girl whose father is interstate will be home next weekend.
- **d** The car which has broken down belongs to Troy.
- **e** My cousin who lives in Adelaide will be visiting us soon.

2 **Combine** the two **simple sentences** into a **complex sentence**. **Underline** the **adjectival clause**.

- **a** The child saw the toys. They were on the shelf.

  ____

- **b** The boy was in the corner. He was quite young.

  ____

3 **Circle** the **relative pronoun** and **underline** the **antecedent**.

- **a** She collected the saddle which was in the tack room.
- **b** My uncle who collects stamps will be in town later.
- **c** Have you seen the caravan that Ching bought?

4 **Write** a sentence using the clause given as an **adjectival clause**.

- **a** who lived in the flat: ______________________________

  ____

- **b** which is near here: ______________________________

  ____

5 **Underline** the **principal clause**. **Mark** a ✓ where the **relative pronoun** is **left out**. **Write** the **relative pronoun**.

- **a** Some of the adults we saw were very sad. ______________
- **b** Are these the goods you ordered? ______________
- **c** In the shed he built he stored the supplies. ______________

6 **Combine** these sentences into a **complex sentence** with the **relative pronoun omitted**.

There is the boat. I bought it yesterday.

____

7 **Underline** the **adjectival clause**. **Circle** the **preposition** that comes **before** the **relative pronoun**.

- **a** I noticed the pond into which many articles had been thrown.
- **b** The teacher of whom I spoke is at a meeting.
- **c** Some cupboards in which the robes were placed were left unlocked.

8 Use *in which she wrote* as an **adjectival clause**.

____

____

☞ Answers on page 123

Section test 3C

9 **Underline** the **adverbial clauses**. **Indicate** whether they are telling **how**, **when**, **where** or **why**.

a He struggled on as if he was very tired. ______________

b When the visitors left we all went to the theatre. ______________

c The athletes gathered where the signs had been set up. ______________

d Phoebe was early because she needed to start straightaway. ______________

e They came home for there was a severe hailstorm. ______________

10 **Add** an **adverbial clause** beginning with the words in **bold**. Write the **type** of **adverbial clause** in the brackets.

a It would not be done **because** ____

______________________________________. (________________)

b **When** ____

he left the village. (________________)

11 **Underline** the **adverbial clauses** and **circle** the **words beginning** them.

a Bridget is much stronger than her sister is.

b The lion struggled hard so that he could release himself.

c Though he was weary he continued on.

12 **Use** the following as **adverbial clauses** in **complex sentences**.

a although it is difficult: ____

____

b if he sees the rubbish: ____

____

13 **Underline** the **noun clauses** and indicate if they are acting as **subject**, **object** or **complement**.

a What he had really learned I do not know. ______________

b What he had really learned is unknown. ______________

c The problem to answer was what he had really learned. ______________

14 **Add** suitable **noun clauses** to **complete** these sentences.

a Why ____ is a mystery.

b She was told that ____.

c Her belief was that ____.

15 **Read** the sentence and answer **yes** or **no** to the statements.

The rumour that the family had left the district was known throughout the area.

The rumour was known throughout the area is the **principal clause**. Yes ☐ No ☐ *(tick)*

The **subordinate clause** is an **adjectival clause**. Yes ☐ No ☐

that the family had left the district is a **noun clause** in **apposition** with *rumour*. Yes ☐ No ☐

☞ Answers on page 123

Review test 3

1 **Underline** the **adjectival phrases** and **circle** the words they **describe**.

a There is a large crate of attractive toys.

b Can you find the book without a cover?

c The flowers in full bloom were near the shed.

2 **Add** a suitable **adjectival phrase** to **describe** the words in **bold**.

a The **dog** ______________________________ scampered away.

b I found the **coat** ______________________________.

c All the **oranges** ______________________________ were ready to pick.

3 **Underline** the **adverbial phrases** and **circle** the **verbs** they **describe**.

a All of the team members played on the new court.

b The water container was left by the fence.

c In the evening take it away.

4 **Add** a suitable **adverbial phrase** to describe the words in **bold**.

a The large box **was found** ______________________________.

b ______________________________ the children always **meet**.

c Do your **work** ______________________________.

5 **Write sentences** using *at the stable* in the following ways.

a adjectival phrase describing *saddle*: ______________________________

____

b adverbial phrase telling us **where**: ______________________________

____

6 **Read** the sentences. Answer **yes** or **no** to the statements.

a Riding the waves was her greatest pleasure.

Riding the waves is a **verbal noun phrase** used as a **subject**. Yes ☐ No ☐ *(tick)*

b All the people were capable of repairing the fence.

repairing the fence is a **verbal noun phrase** used as the **object** of a **preposition**. Yes ☐ No ☐ *(tick)*

7 **Add** suitable **verbal noun phrases**.

a Hamish enjoys ______________________________.

b His uncle is very good at ______________________________.

8 **Use** the following phrases in **sentences**.

a *to clean the bath* as an **infinitive phrase** used as **subject**:

____

b *broken in half* as a **participle phrase** referring to the noun *mast*:

____

☞ Answers on page 123

Review test 3

9 **Identify** the **simple sentences** as stating a **fact**, **opinion** or **possibility**.

a Sharon has ridden here many times. ________________

b Either Jan or Ellen will finish the work. ________________

c Here is the most untidy room. ________________

10 Are these sentences **commands** or **exclamatory sentences**?

a Collect the books early. ________________

b What a good idea! ________________

c Leave it there. ________________

11 Write an **interrogative sentence** beginning with *what*.

____

12 **Change** these sentences into a **compound sentence** using one of the conjunctions *or*, *and* or *but*.

Some of the people went there. None of them ever returned.

____

13 **Read** the sentences. **Identify** the clauses as **principal**, **adjectival**, **adverbial** or **noun**.

a There is the wagon ________________

which had been repaired ________________

because the axle had been broken. ________________

b After you paint the side of the shed ________________

which you were shown ________________

you will be paid immediately. ________________

c That she had made a mistake ________________

became very clear ________________

when the item was assembled ________________

because the lid would not fit. ________________

14 Is this sentence a **compound-complex** sentence? **Explain** your answer.

We will take the trail bikes and travel to the mountain when the starter has advised us. Yes ☐ No ☐ *(tick)*

____

15 Use *although he was careful* as an **adverbial clause** in a sentence with **three clauses**.

____

____

16 **Complete** the **noun clauses** beginning with the word in **bold**.

a **Where** ________________________________ I cannot work out.

b The fact **that** ________________________________ had only just been discovered.

☞ Answers on pages 123–124

4 Syntax and correct usage

Matching nouns and verbs – Rule 1

When we use a **singular subject**, we use a **singular verb**.

- A **singular subject** is used when we are talking about **only one person** or **thing**.
- The **verb** that goes with it must also be **singular**.

Examples

- **His friend** (singular subject) **was leaving** (singular verb) late.

Hint: Always focus on the **subject** and ask yourself whether it is **just one person** or **thing**. If it is, then it must have a **verb** that also **refers** to **one thing**.

- That dog (singular subject) were barking (plural verb) loudly. (INCORRECT)

  In this sentence, *dog* is the **actual subject**. As *dog* is a **singular subject**, it must be **matched** with a **singular verb** and not a plural verb.
- **That dog** (singular subject) **was barking** (singular verb) loudly. (CORRECT)

- Her mother (singular subject) are talking (plural verb) loudly. (INCORRECT)

  In this sentence, *mother* is the **actual subject**. As *mother* is a **singular subject**, it must be **matched** with a **singular verb** and not a **plural verb**.
- **Her mother** (singular subject) **is talking** (singular verb) loudly. (CORRECT)

Are these sentences **correct**? If so, **tick** the **box**. If not, **cross out** the incorrect part and **write** the **corrected part**.

1 Michael have spoken to him. ☐ ____________

2 They was collecting the fruit. ☐ ____________

3 His uncle has brought the parcel. ☐ ____________

4 Mary was waiting at the gate. ☐ ____________

5 Her sister Adele were by the creek. ☐ ____________

6 My cousin are sailing on the lake. ☐ ____________

Answers on page 124

Matching nouns and verbs – Rule 2

When a **collective noun** is the **subject**, we use a **singular verb**.

- **Collective nouns** are used to **name groups** of **things** (e.g. *a* ***mob*** *of cattle, a* ***flock*** *of sheep*), so the things are **referred to** as **just one thing**.
- The **verb** that goes with it must also be **singular**.

Examples

- The **fleet** of ships (singular subject, collective noun) **was sailing** away. (singular verb)

Hint: Find the **subject**. If it is a **singular** word, you must use a **verb** that **refers to only one thing**.

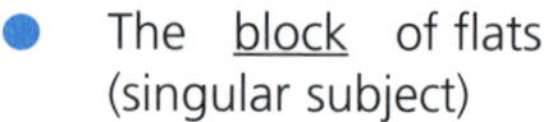

- The block of flats (singular subject) were being built. (plural verb) (INCORRECT)

  In this sentence, *block* is the **actual subject**. As *block* is a **singular subject**, it must be **matched** with a **singular verb** and not a plural verb.

- The **block** of flats (singular subject) **was being built**. (singular verb) (CORRECT)

- The hand of bananas (singular subject) were (plural verb) on the table. (INCORRECT)

  The word *hand* is the **actual subject**. As *hand* is a **singular subject** it must be **matched** with a **singular verb**. The sentence should read:

- The **hand** of bananas (singular subject) **was** (singular verb) on the table. (CORRECT)

Are these sentences **correct**? If so, **tick** the **box**. If not, **cross out** the incorrect part and **write** the **corrected part**.

1 The group of islands are seen from the hill. ☐ ____________

2 A large grove of trees was being watered. ☐ ____________

3 Her bunch of flowers was in the vase. ☐ ____________

4 The list of names were on the table. ☐ ____________

5 A swarm of insects has entered the house. ☐ ____________

6 The litter of pigs were in the pen. ☐ ____________

Answers on page 124

Matching nouns and verbs – Rule 3

When we use a **plural subject**, we use a **plural verb form**.

- A **plural subject** is one where we are talking about **more than one person** or **thing**.
- The **verb** that goes with it must also be **plural**.

Examples

- **David and Elise** (plural subject) **are collecting** (plural verb) the mail.

Hint: The **subject** is made up of **two nouns** (*David* and *Elise*) making a **plural subject**. When this occurs, we must have a **verb** that also **refers to more than one person** or **thing**.

- My two cousins (plural subject) has been (singular verb) there before. (INCORRECT)

  In this sentence, *cousins* is the **actual subject**. As *cousins* is a **plural subject**, it must be **matched** to a **plural verb**.

- **My two cousins** (plural subject) **have been** (plural verb) there before. (CORRECT)

- Jason and his sister (plural subject) was leaving (singular verb) the park. (INCORRECT)

  In this sentence, *Jason* and *sister* are the **actual subject words**. These words make up a **plural subject** and must be **matched** to a **plural verb**, not a singular verb.

- **Jason and his sister** (plural subject) **were leaving** (plural verb) the park. (CORRECT)

Are these sentences **correct**? If so, **tick** the **box**. If not, **cross out** the incorrect part and **write** the **corrected part**.

1 Mike and Eloise has visited the show. ☐ ____________

2 His uncle and aunt are attending the party. ☐ ____________

3 Her brothers, Luke and Ray, have passed the test. ☐ ____________

4 Laura, Paula and Claire was seen at the shop. ☐ ____________

5 The young children are reading the books. ☐ ____________

6 Several girls and boys has played the game. ☐ ____________

Answers on page 124

Matching nouns and verbs – Rule 4

When **two subjects** are **joined** by *with* or *as well as*, the **verb** must **match** the **subject word** before *with* or *as well as*.

- In the sentences below, we may use a **singular or plural verb**.
- If the subject word before *with* or *as well as* is **singular**, the **verb** must be **singular**.
- If the subject word before *with* or *as well as* is **plural**, the **verb** must be **plural**.

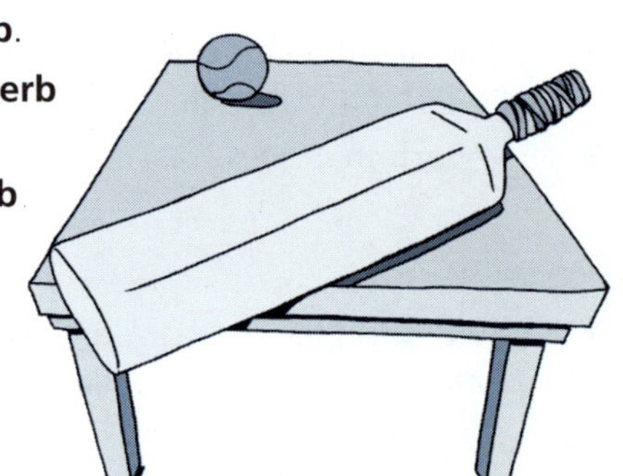

Examples

- The **bat** with the ball (singular subject word) **is** on the table. (singular verb)

Hint: The **subject** of the sentence is actually *The bat with the ball*. The **subject word** before *with* is a **singular word**, so the **verb** must be **singular**.

- The girls as well as the boys (plural subject word) has visited the farm. (singular verb) (INCORRECT)

  In this sentence, *girls* is the word before *as well as* and is a **plural subject word**, so we need a **plural verb**.

- The **girls** as well as the boys (plural subject word) **have** visited the farm. (plural verb) (CORRECT)

- The car with the caravan (singular subject) were on the road. (plural verb) (INCORRECT)

  In this sentence, *car* is the word before *with*. The word *car* is a **singular subject word** so we need a **singular verb**.

- The **car** with the caravan (singular subject) **was** on the road. (singular verb) (CORRECT)

Are these sentences **correct**? If so, **tick** the **box**. If not, **cross out** the incorrect part and **write** the **corrected part**.

1 The cat with its master is at the show. ☐ ____________

2 Elephants as well as lions were drinking at the lake. ☐ ____________

3 The cakes with the biscuits are on the table. ☐ ____________

4 James as well as his father have been there. ☐ ____________

5 The cups with the saucers were broken as well. ☐ ____________

6 Players with their equipment were boarding the aircraft. ☐ ____________

☞ Answers on page 124

Matching pronouns and verbs – Rule 5

When we use the **pronouns** *each*, *either*, *neither*, *anybody* and *nobody* they must be **matched** to a **singular verb**.

When used as pronouns, *each*, *either*, *neither*, *anybody* and *nobody* are all **singular words**. They then need a **singular verb** to **match** them.

Examples

- **Each** of the boys (singular pronoun subject) **has finished** (singular verb) the work.

Hint: The words *each*, *either* and *neither* will often be followed by a phrase such as *of the boys*, but the **verb** must be **singular** to match *each*, *either* and *neither*.

- Neither of the girls (singular pronoun subject) have been (plural verb) there. (INCORRECT)

  The simple subject is *neither* and as it is a **singular pronoun**, a **singular verb** is required.

- **Neither** of the girls (singular pronoun subject) **has been** (singular verb) there. (CORRECT)

- Nobody (singular pronoun subject) were finished (plural verb) before the bell. (INCORRECT)

  The word *nobody* is the **actual subject word** and is a **singular pronoun**. It must be **matched** to a **singular verb**.

- **Nobody** (singular pronoun subject) **was finished** (singular verb) before the bell. (CORRECT)

Are these sentences **correct**? If so, **tick** the **box**. If not, **cross out** the incorrect part and **write** the **corrected part**.

1 Neither of the cars were damaged. ☐ ____________

2 Each of the ponies is trotting away. ☐ ____________

3 Either of the boys were absent. ☐ ____________

4 Anybody were able to finish it. ☐ ____________

5 Nobody was at the gate at all. ☐ ____________

6 Each have won a good prize. ☐ ____________

Answers on page 124

Section test 4A

1 **Read** the sentences below. **Refer to** the **five matching subject** and **verb rules**. **Which rule** needs to be followed to **correct** the sentences?

		Rule number
a	Neither of the athletes have entered the event.	________
b	Jo and Lisa has brought in the parcel.	________
c	The flock of sheep are in the paddock.	________
d	Milton have yet to finish the work.	________
e	A car as well as a van are in the yard.	________

2 Now **rewrite** the **sentences** above in the correct form. **Underline** the **corrections**.

a ____

b ____

c ____

d ____

e ____

3 **Read** these sentences and **insert** the correct form of the **verb** in brackets in the spaces.

a My friend Shania ____________ completed the work. (*has*, *have*)

b John and Cass ____________ preparing the work. (*is*, *are*)

c The flock of birds ____________ flown across the paddock. (*has*, *have*)

d Neither of the twins ____________ playing in the creek. (*was*, *were*)

e Somebody ____________ stolen the valuable watch. (*has*, *have*)

4 **Check** these sentences. Are they correct? If not, **cross out** the incorrect words and **write** the **corrected part** in the brackets.

a Several cars was held up at the bridge. (________________)

b A number of small objects were in the purse. (________________)

c Each girl has done her work well. (________________)

d Neither of the men have won the event. (________________)

e The clock as well as the whistle are in the box. (________________)

5 **Insert** a correct **compound verb**, either **singular** or **plural**, to complete these sentences.

a Miriam ____________________ the work early.

b The artists in the group ____________________ their latest works.

c Either Joe or Sharnie ____________________ the parcel.

d The horse as well as the pony ____________________ into the stable.

e A pride of lions ____________________ down close to the trees.

☞ Answers on page 124

Comparative and superlative degrees – Rule 6

When **two things** are being **referred to**, we use the **comparative degree** of the **adjective** and for **more than two things**, we use the **superlative degree**.

- **Adjectives** are **describing words**.
- When an adjective is used to compare **two persons** or **things**, we use the **comparative degree**.
- When an adjective is used to compare **more than two** persons or things, we use the **superlative degree**.
- **large** ➡ **larger** (comparative) ➡ **largest** (superlative)

Examples

- This car is **<u>older</u>** than the truck.

  Here we are **comparing two things**, so we use the **comparative**.
- Here is the **<u>oldest</u>** vehicle in the car yard.

  Here we are **comparing more than two things**, so we use the **superlative**.

- The horse is the <u>fastest</u> of the two. (INCORRECT)
  (superlative degree)

  In this sentence, we are **comparing just two horses**. We should be using the **comparative degree**.
- This horse is the **<u>faster</u>** of the two. (CORRECT)
  (comparative degree)

- This rope is the <u>longer</u> of all the ropes. (INCORRECT)
  (comparative degree)

  In this sentence, we are **comparing more than two ropes**. We should be using the **superlative degree**.
- This rope is the **<u>longest</u>** of all the ropes. (CORRECT)
  (superlative degree)

Are these sentences **correct**? If so, **tick the box**. If not, **cross out** the incorrect part and **write** the **corrected part**.

1. This is the brightest star in the sky. ☐ ____________
2. Of all the children, Alan is the faster runner. ☐ ____________
3. Is this the prettiest work of the two on the wall? ☐ ____________
4. That is the angriest lioness in the pride. ☐ ____________
5. The bigger fish from the catch was taken away. ☐ ____________
6. Tim has the larger collection in the class. ☐ ____________

☞ Answers on page 124

Comparative and superlative degrees – Rule 7

When **two things** are **being compared**, the words *more* or *less* are used to make the **comparative degree** of the **adjective**, and the words *most* or *least* are used for the **superlative degree**.

- This rule applies to **adjectives** that **cannot use** *er* or *est* for the **comparative** and **superlative degrees**.
- tidy ➡ tidi**er** ➡ tidi**est**
- beautiful ➡ **more** beautiful ➡ **most** beautiful

  ➡ **less** beautiful ➡ **least** beautiful

Examples

- She is a <u>**more careful**</u> driver than her sister.
  (comparative degree)

  In this sentence, we are **comparing** two drivers. It would be awkward to add *er* to *careful*, so we use *more* to form the **comparative degree**.

- This is the <u>**most dangerous**</u> road in the district.
  (superlative degree)

  Here we are **comparing many roads**. It would be awkward to add *est* to *dangerous*, so we use *most* to form the **superlative degree**.

- Saturday was the <u>most enjoyable</u> day of the weekend. (INCORRECT)
  (superlative degree)

  In this sentence, we are really **comparing** only **two days**, Saturday and Sunday. We should be using the **comparative degree**.

- Saturday was the <u>**more enjoyable**</u> day of the weekend. (CORRECT)
  (comparative degree)

- Sally is the <u>more agreeable</u> of the five girls. (INCORRECT)
  (comparative degree)

  Here we are **comparing more than two girls**. We should be using the **superlative degree**.

- Sally is the <u>**most agreeable**</u> of the five girls. (CORRECT)
  (superlative degree)

Are these sentences **correct**? If so, **tick** the **box**. If not, **cross out** the incorrect part and **write** the **corrected part**.

1 It was the most splendid palace of the two. ☐ ________
2 This animal is the most fierce of the predators. ☐ ________
3 Climate here is more pleasant than in that area. ☐ ________
4 She created the more horrible mask of anyone in her class. ☐ ________
5 The coat is the most attractive of all. ☐ ________
6 This animal is the more inquisitive of any in the cat family. ☐ ________

Answers on page 124

Using relative pronouns – Rule 8

When we use an **adjectival clause**, the **relative pronoun** must always be placed **as close as possible** to the **antecedent**. When using an **adjectival clause**, the **relative pronouns** *who*, *whom* and *whose* must **refer** to **people**.

- An **adjectival clause** describes a **noun** or **pronoun** in one of the **other clauses** in a **sentence**.
- The **word** it **describes** is called its **antecedent**.
- An **adjectival clause** is **introduced by** a **relative pronoun**.

Examples

- She is a fine **runner** **who** is very consistent.
  (antecedent) (relative pronoun)

  There are two clauses. *She is a fine runner* is the **principal clause** and *who is very consistent* is an **adjectival clause**.

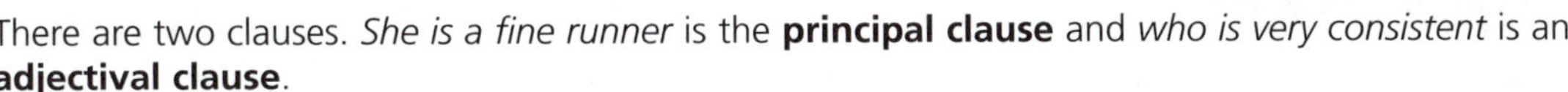

- Jan works in our store on the weekends which is on the corner. (INCORRECT)
  (antecedent) (relative pronoun)

  In this sentence, the **clause** *which is on the corner* is **adjectival**. Its **relative pronoun** needs to be **close** to the **antecedent**.

- Jan works on the weekends in our **store** **which** is on the corner. (CORRECT)
  (antecedent) (relative pronoun)

- Sandy saw the girl that lives nearby. (INCORRECT)
  (antecedent) (relative pronoun)

  The **relative pronoun** used here is *that*. The **antecedent** of the **adjectival clause** is *girl*. The **adjectival clause** is **referring to** a **person**, so the **relative pronoun** must be *who*, *whom* or *whose*.

- Sandy saw the **girl** **who** lives nearby. (CORRECT)
  (antecedent) (relative pronoun)

Are these sentences **correct**? If so, **tick** the **box**. If not, **rewrite** them **correctly**.

1. I live in the street near you which leads to Warra.
   ☐ ______________________________
2. There is the cat that lives in the old house.
   ☐ ______________________________
3. She crept along the stairs to the room that had a damaged railing.
   ☐ ______________________________
4. Did you see the adult that collected the mail?
   ☐ ______________________________

Answers on pages 124–125

Auxiliary verb and past participle – Rule 9

When an **auxiliary verb** is used, we add a **past participle** with it and not the past tense of the verb.

- Auxiliary verbs are helping verbs.
- When we use a helping verb, such as *has*, *have* or *had*, we use the **past participle** of the **main verb** with it.

Examples

Main verb: *eat* (present tense) *eating* (present participle)
ate (past tense) *eaten* (past participle)

- The people **have** **eaten** the vegetables.
  (auxiliary verb) (past participle of main verb **eat**)

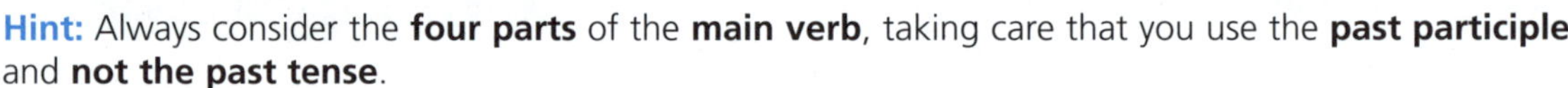

Hint: Always consider the **four parts** of the **main verb**, taking care that you use the **past participle** and **not the past tense**.

- The job has been did well. (INCORRECT)
  (auxiliary verb) (past tense)

  In this sentence, the **past tense** of the **main verb** *do* has been used instead of the past participle *done*.

  do (present tense) *doing* (present participle)

  did (past tense) *done* (past participle)

- The job **has been** **done** well. (CORRECT)
  (auxiliary verb) (past participle)

- Has the boy came home yet? (INCORRECT)
  (auxiliary verb) (past tense)

  We have used the **past tense** of the verb *came* instead of the past participle.

  come (present tense) *coming* (present participle)

  came (past tense) *come* (past participle)

- **Has** the boy **come** home yet? (CORRECT)
  (auxiliary verb) (past participle)

Are these sentences **correct**? If so, **tick** the **box**. If not, **cross out** the incorrect part and **write** the **corrected part**.

1 The boy has rode that horse before. ❑ ________
2 The young girls have drove the car into the creek. ❑ ________
3 Has he fallen yet? ❑ ________
4 The strong winds have blew for many hours. ❑ ________
5 The girl has hid the parcel under the bed. ❑ ________
6 Miriam and I have sang the song. ❑ ________

Answers on page 125

Participle phrases – Rule 10

When a **participle** is **used on its own**, it must **refer** to **something**.

- When we look at **verbs**, we **distinguish between present tense**, **past tense**, **past participle** and **present participle**. For example:

  know (present tense) *knew* (past tense)

  knowing (present participle) *known* (past participle)

- The **past** and **present participles** are often used to begin **participle phrases**. These phrases must **refer** to **someone** or **something**.

Examples

- **Having** started the work (present participle) **we** found the painting easy. (the word to which the participle refers)

  The **participle phrase** must have a word to which it can **refer**. The **participle** *having* refers to the pronoun *we*.

- Travelling (participle) by train, the country looked beautiful. (INCORRECT)

  In this sentence, the **participle** has no word to which it can refer. It **does not refer** to the word *country*, so the sentence must be rebuilt.

- **Travelling** (participle) by train, **we** (the word to which the participle refers) noticed the country looked beautiful. (CORRECT)

- Seeing (participle) the car, the matter was reported to the police. (INCORRECT)

  Again, the **participle does not refer** to any other word in the sentence. The sentence needs to be rebuilt so that it **contains** a **referring word**.

- **Seeing** (participle) the car, **they** (the word to which the participle refers) reported the matter to the police. (CORRECT)

Are these sentences **correct**? If so, **tick** the **box**. If not, **rewrite** them **correctly**.

1 Following at a safe distance, the fog confused us.

☐ ____________________

2 Blown by the wind, the going was difficult.

☐ ____________________

3 Having visited the cave, the journey took three hours.

☐ ____________________

4 The boys, singing loudly, came across a large waterhole.

☐ ____________________

☞ Answers on page 125

Section test 4B

1 **Read** the sentences below. **Refer** to Rules 6–10. Which **rule** needs to be followed to **correct** the sentences?

		Rule number
a	This is the more pleasant colour of the four you selected.	________
b	All of them have came here before.	________
c	Here is the sharper pencil of the six on the desk.	________
d	Walking along the path, the wildflowers looked pretty.	________
e	Mary saw the girl which had been in the street.	________

2 Now **rewrite** the **sentences** above in correct form. **Underline** the **corrections**.

a ____

b ____

c ____

d ____

e ____

3 **Read** these sentences. In the spaces **insert** the **correct form** of the **adjective**, **relative pronoun** or **verb** from the brackets.

a It is the ______________ race course in the country. (*longer*, *longest*)

b Here is the young rider ____________ lives next door. (*who*, *whose*, *which*)

c Have the children ________________ the glasses? (*broke*, *broken*)

d There was the ____________________ rose in the display on the table. (*more beautiful*, *most beautiful*)

e The material had ________________ in the wash. (*shrank*, *shrunk*)

4 **Check** the following sentences. Are they **correct**? If not, **cross out** the incorrect words and **rewrite** the **corrected part** in the brackets.

a The climb to the summit is the most dangerous in the district. (__________________)

b I found the small creature who had been injured. (__________________)

c The stranger item in the huge collection was brightly coloured. (__________________)

d Watching the flock, the shepherd finally fell asleep. (__________________)

e Has the boy rang the bell yet? (__________________)

5 **Add** a suitable **word** to complete the sentences according to the **rule indicated**.

a (Rule 6) Here is the ______________________ item in the store.

b (Rule 7) This is the ______________________ of the two paintings.

c (Rule 8) Samantha saw the girl ________________ danced in the contest.

d (Rule 9) Have the children ________________ the food yet?

e (Rule 10) Looking at the pool, ________________ noticed the branches under the surface.

Answers on page 125

Correct verb usage 1

Before starting this section, re-read Chapter 1, pages 15–17. In this section, we are revisiting **tense** and **participles**. The common verbs we will look at here are called **irregular verbs**. Also, look again at Rule 9 (page 86).

	Present tense	Past tense	Past participle	Present participle
1	arise	arose	arisen	arising
2	begin	began	begun	beginning
3	blow	blew	blown	blowing
4	break	broke	broken	breaking
5	choose	chose	chosen	choosing
6	do	did	done	doing
7	draw	drew	drawn	drawing
8	know	knew	known	knowing

Complete the following sentences using the **correct forms** of the **verbs** from the table above. (Use verb 1 for question 1, and so on.)

1 **a** All the children ________________ at seven o'clock.
b When they had ________________, they set out for the farm.
c On ________________ early the explorers packed their gear.

2 **a** The work was ________________ as early as possible.
b Gideon ________________ to collect the timber yesterday.
c Will you ________________ the work now please.

3 **a** The wind ________________ strongly from the east.
b That huge tree was ________________ down in the storm.
c The upper air ________________ in from the west caused a drop in temperature.

4 **a** The waves will ________________ over the damaged vessel.
b The glass was ________________ when it hit the floor.
c She heard a dull ________________ sound.

5 **a** Mila will ________________ a new top for the summer holidays.
b Many of them took part but few were ________________ to represent the school.
c Did you ________________ a new novel to read?

6 **a** Has all the work been ________________ correctly?
b ________________ you see the new sports car by the road?
c She has been ________________ this work all day.

7 **a** The artist ________________ the sketch by lunchtime.
b Has she ________________ any money from her account?
c My sister ________________ the rough map in the sand.

8 **a** He had ________________ where the people had gone for some time.
b All the visitors ________________ what the presents were.

☞ Answers on page 125

Correct verb usage 2

Again, **study** the **four parts** of the **common verbs** below.

	Present tense	Past tense	Past participle	Present participle
1	drink	drank	drunk	drinking
2	drive	drove	driven	driving
3	fall	fell	fallen	falling
4	fly	flew	flown	flying
5	give	gave	given	giving
6	hide	hid	hidden	hiding
7	lay (lay an egg)	laid	laid	laying
8	lie (tell a lie)	lied	lied	lying
9	lie (to rest or recline)	lay	lain	lying

Complete the following sentences using the **correct forms** of the **verbs** from the table above. (Use verb 1 for question 1, and so on.)

1 **a** The children __________________ the water thirstily.
b All the travellers had __________________ from the well.
c Do not __________________ all the water in the container.

2 **a** The car was __________________ towards the nearby township.
b The riders __________________ the cattle along the track.
c After __________________ for several hours, she was very tired.

3 **a** Some of the fittings had __________________ onto the floor.
b The young rider __________________ from the young colt.
c Be careful not to __________________ into those potholes.

4 **a** The birds had __________________ in from the far west.
b Was the kite __________________ over the house?

5 **a** The presents had been __________________ to all the relatives.
b The child __________________ the stamps to his brother.
c After __________________ away the toys, Grant left the room.

6 **a** All the money had been __________________ in the hollow log.
b Josie __________________ from her sister in the small cupboard.

7 – **9**
a The small bird has __________________ three eggs in the nest.
b Rebecca was __________________ on the bed on the veranda.
c She had __________________ on the sofa for several hours.
d The young boy __________________ to his mother about the missing money.
e All the hens had __________________ during the early part of the day.
f Has he __________________ about the stolen goods again?
g Tania __________________ down under the shady tree.
h Has the injured child __________________ on the stretcher for long?

Answers on page 125

Correct verb usage 3

Again, **study** the **four parts** of the **common verbs** below. Beneath them are sets of sentences to be **completed**.

	Present tense	Past tense	Past participle	Present participle
1	ride	rode	ridden	riding
2	ring	rang	rung	ringing
3	rise	rose	risen	rising
4	see	saw	seen	seeing
5	show	showed	shown	showing
6	shrink	shrank	shrunk	shrinking
7	sing	sang	sung	singing
8	sink	sank	sunk	sinking

Complete the following sentences using the **correct forms** of the **verbs** from the table above. (Use verb 1 for question 1, and so on.)

1 **a** All the children had __________________ on the train.
b Daniel __________________ the young filly in the event.
c The boy __________________ the Arab mare is my brother.

2 **a** She __________________ the bell at the correct time.
b Has Sean __________________ the alarm in the office?
c The huge bell was __________________ loudly across the area.

3 **a** The animal __________________ up on its back legs and attacked.
b The sun had __________________ before seven o'clock recently.
c The moon __________________ slowly in the northern sky.

4 **a** Many of them are __________________ the play for the first time.
b Have you __________________ these creatures before?
c __________________ the strange sight, the dog ran for cover.

5 **a** They were __________________ their friends the new vehicle.
b I __________________ my uncle the model car I made.
c They had __________________ everybody the famous artwork.

6 **a** The material __________________ badly in the wash.
b The rope dried out and had __________________ by at least three centimetres.
c The area of useful land was __________________ because of the salt problem.

7 **a** Jenny __________________ the song beautifully.
b She had __________________ the popular song many times.
c The choir was __________________ at the local shopping centre.

8 **a** The small boat __________________ quickly after it struck the rock.
b Several ships have __________________ in these dangerous waters.
c I saw the bird __________________ beneath the waves.

Answers on page 125

Correct verb usage 4

This is the final exercise on the use of the **four parts** of **common verbs**. Beneath them are sets of sentences to be **completed**.

	Present tense	Past tense	Past participle	Present participle
1	speak	spoke	spoken	speaking
2	spring	sprang	sprung	springing
3	steal	stole	stolen	stealing
4	swim	swam	swum	swimming
5	take	took	taken	taking
6	tear	tore	torn	tearing
7	throw	threw	thrown	throwing
8	write	wrote	written	writing

Complete the following sentences using the **correct forms** of the **verbs** from the table above. (Use verb 1 for question 1, and so on.)

1 a Many of my relatives have ________________ to the musician.
b Do not ________________ so loudly in this small room.
c Skye ________________ to her sisters almost every day.

2 a The small craft had ________________ a leak on the journey.
b All the animals ________________ into the dense forest.
c ________________ forward, the lioness advanced on its prey.

3 a The boy said that he did not ________________ the goods.
b Was the precious vase ________________ during the night?
c The intruders ________________ all the pieces of jewellery.

4 a Can you ________________ across the lake to the village?
b Lainey has ________________ in this pool every day this week.
c Stevie ________________ in the deep rock pool for hours.

5 a Has Tracey ________________ the netball gear to the storeroom?
b My sister ________________ all the books back to the library.
c Do not ________________ any of the money on the table.

6 a The chart had been ________________ from the wall.
b Joe ________________ his shirt during the game on the oval.
c Try not to ________________ that new piece of material.

7 a The box had been ________________ over the cliff yesterday.
b Can you ________________ the ball into the hoop?
c Marcia has ________________ all of the rubbish out.

8 a Sharon is ________________ a long letter to her friend.
b This document was ________________ years ago.
c Sal ________________ out the story for his friends.

Answers on page 125

Review test 4

1 **Read** each sentence. **Cross out** the incorrect part. **Write** the **corrected part** in the space. (Use Rules 1–5.)

- **a** My sister Ellen and her brother was down at the station. (____________)
- **b** The huge mob of horses have galloped across the plain. (____________)
- **c** The old man by the fence have spoken to him often. (____________)
- **d** His uncle and aunt has travelled there many times. (____________)
- **e** The elephant as well as the tiger were missing from the zoo. (__________)
- **f** A book with a new pen were left on the table. (____________)
- **g** Neither of the animals were resting in the shade. (____________)
- **h** Each of the camels have travelled across the desert. (____________)
- **i** Nobody were able to finish the work before dark. (____________)

2 **Read** each sentence. **Draw a line** through the incorrect part. **Write the corrected part** in the space. (Use Rules 6–10.)

- **a** Of all the colts in the field this is the faster of all. (______________________)
- **b** Is this the neatest work of the two samples you have? (______________________)
- **c** This is the most beautifulest painting I have seen. (______________________)
- **d** Of the two brothers, Eric is the most generous. (______________________)
- **e** The more unusual of the ten sculptures is at the entrance. (______________________)
- **f** Alana is the girl that lives in the next street. (______________________)
- **g** Has young Charlie came home from the concert? (______________________)
- **h** All of the coins and notes were hid in the forest. (______________________)
- **i** They live in a town near you which is close to the foothills.
  (____)
- **j** Running into the distance, it became darker and darker.
  (____)

3 **Select the correct forms** of each of the verbs from the three in brackets. **Write** in the spaces.

- **a** (arise, arose, arisen)
  All of the children ________________ at the same time each day.
- **b** (blow, blown, blowing)
  The sheets of paper had ________________ away in the wind.
- **c** (choose, chose, chosen)
  His elder brother had ________________ the present himself.
- **d** (draw, drew, drawn)
  Did Amy ________________ the picture that is seen on the wall?
- **e** (begin, began, begun)
  The work was ________________ on the farm early in the day.
- **f** (drive, drove, driven)
  Some of the villagers had ________________ for many hours.

Answers on pages 125–126

g (fly, flew, flown)
All of the birds had ________________ across the wasteland.

h (give, gave, given)
The leader of the group ________________ out all the awards.

i (know, known, knowing)
The information collected was not ________________ by the group.

j (lied, lied, lying)
Ahmet had not ________________ to his parents about the missing money.

k (lay, lain, lying)
Suzanne was ________________ on the couch for many hours.

l (ride, rode, ridden)
The stallion is being ________________ quickly across the flat.

m (rise, raise, risen)
The huge balloon has ________________ slowly from the ground.

n (showed, shown, showing)
Jack ________________ all of his toys to his relatives.

o (shrink, shrank, shrunk)
Some of the woollen material will ________________ when wet.

p (sing, song, sung)
This song has been ________________ by the group many times.

q (speak, spoke, spoken)
Have any of you people ________________ to the new dentist?

r (swim, swam, swum)
Last year the players ________________ regularly in the lap pool.

s (tear, tore, torn)
These sheets have been ________________ for some time.

t (throw, threw, thrown)
Mario can ________________ the ball with great accuracy.

u (write, wrote, written)
All the letters were ________________ by his father last week.

4 **Insert** *lie*, *lay*, *laid*, *lain* or *lied* to complete these sentences.

a The child ________________ on the bed for hours.

b The emu will ________________ an egg out on the plain.

c Verity ________________ down for some time.

d 'Do not ________________ to me', the teacher ordered.

Answers on page 126

5 Functional grammar terms and usage

Participants

Participants are the **people**, **places**, **ideas** and **things** that **take part** in the **action** or **discussion** in a sentence.

In most cases, **participants** are **subjects** or **objects**.

Examples

- **The tired old man** (participant) leaned wearily on the fence.
- **All of the children** (participant) collected **the ripe red apples**. (participant)
- **They** (participant) had not bought **the bright red sports car**. (participant)

1 **Underline** the **participants** in these sentences.

- **a** Many of the sailors were on shore leave.
- **b** It has completed thousands of repetitions.
- **c** My young sister Meg has bought some of the plants.
- **d** Have you and your father visited the Jenolan Caves?
- **e** The damaged old building is beyond repair.
- **f** Some green marbles were also sold at the store.

2 **Replace** the **participants** in **bold** in these sentences with ones of your own choice.

- **a** **The agile kitten** climbed up the tree quickly. ____________________
- **b** **Some of the boys** had played for hours in the garden. ____________________
- **c** **The worker** carried **the large boxes** to the truck.

  ____
- **d** **Lots of monkeys** were playing **lively games** in the area.

  ____

3 **Create participants** to **match** the instructions below and **make sentences**. One has been done for you.

- **a** three nouns and one pronoun: ***Jack, Joe and their sister*** *went to the village.*
- **b** two nouns and two adjectives: ____________________
- **c** two pronouns: ____________________

0:00

Quick check

Are the word groups in **bold participants**?

1. Has the girl gone **to the shop**? Yes ☐ No ☐ *(tick)*
2. They collected **the petals** early in the day. Yes ☐ No ☐
3. My sister plays **netball** on the weekend. Yes ☐ No ☐
4. These fine homes have **been built well**. Yes ☐ No ☐

Answers on page 126

Processes

Processes are the **action** or **state** of **being verbs**.

They can be described as **action** verb groups, **thinking** or **feeling** verb groups, **telling** or **saying** verb groups, or **having** or **being** verb groups.

Processes are **verbs** and **verb groups**.

Examples

- The artists **had been painting** the mural.
  (action verb group)
- Josie **had not realised** the danger of the cliffs.
  (thinking or feeling verb group)
- **Could** you **explain** the method to be used?
  (telling or saying verb group)
- The strangers **were not being** very quiet in the store.
  (having or being verb group)

1 **Underline** the **processes** in the following sentences.

a All of the children had been eating the food.

b Did the young boy understand the rules of the game?

c The rider had often spoken to the stablehand.

d Sue has been there at the show many times.

e Sharon will be collecting all the materials today.

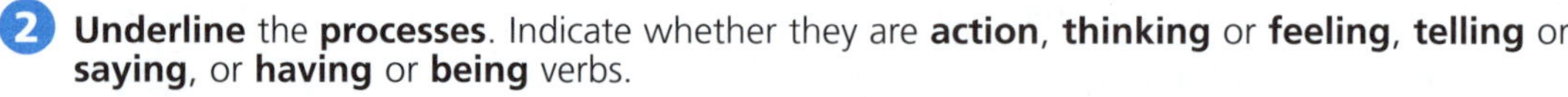

2 **Underline** the **processes**. Indicate whether they are **action**, **thinking** or **feeling**, **telling** or **saying**, or **having** or **being** verbs.

a Has Glen practised for the piano recital?

____

b The young driver did not understand the directions.

____

c Many of them could not identify the strange specimens.

____

d Bobby and Ewan are being very attentive in class.

____

3 **Add processes** of the **type indicated** in brackets to these sentences.

a Many of the writers ________________________ the work early. (action verb)

b Joan and her sister ________________________ the firewood. (action verb)

c Georgina ________________________ the job was well done. (thinking or feeling verb)

d Neither Dan nor Jim ________________________ the way to the shop. (telling or saying verb)

e The mine workers ________________________ very careful in the narrow space. (having or being verb)

☞ Answers on page 126

Attributes

An **attribute** is a word or phrase that **adds** to the **meaning** of a **noun** or **pronoun**. It is an **adjective** or **adjectival phrase**.

Example

- The **tall, athletic** boy became a **fine basketball** player.
  (attributes—adjectives) (attributes)
- This car **with a red roof** is for sale at a **bargain** price.
  (attribute—adjectival phrase) (attribute)

1 **Underline** the **attributes** in these sentences. **Circle** the words to which they **refer**.

- **a** Many outdated machines were rusting in the shed.
- **b** The burning sun shone down on the brightly coloured boats.
- **c** The oval by the creek has been flooded badly.
- **d** Oscar has twenty brand-new felt pens.
- **e** The New South Wales team was a very strong one.
- **f** Those fish from South America are quite rare.

2 **Circle** the **participants** and **underline** the **attributes** in these sentences.

- **a** We waited at the narrow entrance to the school hall.
- **b** In the dense jungle the small boy lost his way.
- **c** Those juicy oranges should be in the refrigerator.
- **d** Happy memories of joyous days came back to the old man.
- **e** The woman removed the pan from the hot stove.
- **f** A framework of steel was erected for the building.

3 **Circle** the **attributes** and **underline** the **processes** in these sentences.

- **a** The announcer's loud voice was heard clearly from afar.
- **b** The young boy sick from the pain went to bed.
- **c** All day long through the village sounded the tread of marching men.
- **d** Never have I seen him before.
- **e** Numerous glittering stones were selected by the buyer.

4 **Circle** the **noun groups** in these sentences and **underline** any **attributes**.

- **a** I followed the long winding tracks and trails to the river.
- **b** The boys and girls with exceptional talent in ball games were selected.
- **c** The competitions and tournaments in the park went on for hours.

Quick check

Add suitable **attributes** to the following sentences.

1 The ______________________ foal was in the high paddock.

2 She was able to complete the ______________________ painting.

3 That ______________________ tree ______________________ was cut down recently.

Answers on page 126

Circumstances

Circumstances are words or phrases that **tell us how**, **when**, **where** or **why**. They are **adverbs** or **adverbial phrases**.

Examples

- Many of them struggled (process) **constantly**. (circumstance)
- The box was placed (process) **in the cupboard**. (circumstance)

1 **Underline** the **circumstances** in these sentences. **Circle** the **processes** they **modify**.

a There in the distance was an old abandoned castle.

b At dusk the animals moved towards the lake.

c Across the burning sands the camel caravan moved slowly.

d With great speed the rocket blasted into space.

e Carefully the actor prepared his costume.

2 **Circle** the **participants** and **underline** the **circumstances** in these sentences.

a Many of the young children played in the yard.

b Slowly and carefully he removed the small block of metal.

c Has she been to the fair lately?

d Bryn and Janie frequently played tennis on that court.

e For no reason the young filly trotted out of the yard.

3 **Use** the following as **circumstances** in sentences of your own. **Underline** the **processes** that are **modified**.

a *later, in the showground*:

____

b *sometimes, at dawn*:

____

c *by the shed, towards evening*:

____

4 **Use** the following **circumstances** with the **forms** of the **verb** listed.

a *seldom*, action verb group:

____

b *immediately*, thinking or feeling verb group:

____

c *by daylight*, telling or saying verb group:

____

d *in reasonable time*, having or being verb group:

____

Answers on page 126

Section test 5A

1. **Underline** the **participants** in these sentences.
   - **a** Some of the animals were taken to the zoo.
   - **b** The machine had processed hundreds of metal frames.
   - **c** Has Charles completed the craft work yet?
   - **d** My cousin Emma works in the old wool stores.
   - **e** Many small bolts were collected during the day.

2. **a** **Use** *the old sea-captain* as a **participant** in a sentence.

   ____

   b **Use** *a bottle of water* as a **participant** in a sentence.

   ____

3. **Underline** the **processes** in the following sentences.
   - **a** She has been cleaning the bathroom basin.
   - **b** Did the rider leave his saddle here?
   - **c** They were displaying all the new artwork.
   - **d** Selma might have been walking along the cliff.

4. **Underline** the **processes**. Indicate whether they are **action**, **thinking** or **feeling**, **telling** or **saying**, or **having** or **being** verbs.
   - **a** Has Martin polished the new table yet?

     ____
   - **b** Marie and Ekin were listening very carefully.

     ____
   - **c** Could you repeat that last sentence?

     ____

5. **Circle** the **attributes** in these sentences. **Underline** the words to which they **refer**.
   - **a** Into the steamy dense jungle the explorers vanished.
   - **b** Many tall young athletes trained at the park.
   - **c** He saw some strong experienced lifters in the competition.

6. **Use** *a rare, beautiful, handmade* as an **attribute** in a **sentence**.

   ____

7. **Underline** the **circumstances**. **Circle** the **processes** to which they **refer**.
   - **a** Some of the girls played quietly in the yard.
   - **b** There in the middle of the park rested the tired runner.
   - **c** Seldom has he been able to find the easiest path.
   - **d** Into the dust and beyond the mountains the travellers journeyed.

☞ Answers on page 127

Mood

Mood is a term we use to **show how** a **process (verb) is used** in a sentence.

There are **three moods**:

- **Indicative** mood (used to express a **fact**)
- **Imperative** mood (used to express a **command**)
- **Subjunctive** mood (used to express **hopes**, **wishes** or **uncertainty**)

Examples

- There **are** many people here. (statement ➡ **indicative** mood)
- **Collect** those parcels. (command ➡ **imperative** mood)
- I wish I **collected** stamps. (wish ➡ **subjunctive** mood)

1 Read the sentences and **identify** them as **indicative**, **imperative** or **subjunctive mood**.

a Take the parcel to his place. ____________

b Many of them attended the concert. ____________

c If only the travellers had taken enough water. ____________

d Go with them to the waterhole. ____________

e She does really enjoy ice skating. ____________

2 **Add** a suitable **verb** of the **mood shown** to these sentences.

a ____________ useful at least once a day. (imperative)

b They ____________ using a lot of the material. (indicative)

c How I wish that it ____________ Friday. (subjunctive)

d ____________ some more of this delicious cake. (imperative)

e I hope we ____________ to the movies tomorrow. (subjunctive)

3 **Use** the **verb** and **mood** shown to **create** your own **sentence**.

a *raced*; indicative:

____

b *leave*; imperative:

____

c *doubt*; subjunctive:

____

4 **Identify** the **mood** of the **verbs** in **bold** and state whether they are **action**, **thinking** or **feeling**, **telling** or **saying**, or **having** or **being** verbs.

a The circus **is coming** to town tomorrow.

Mood: ____________ Form of verb: ____________

b Please **collect** all the paper from the table.

Mood: ____________ Form of verb: ____________

c I sincerely trust you **visit** us again.

Mood: ____________ Form of verb: ____________

☞ Answers on page 127

Theme and rheme

The **theme** is the **first part** of a **clause** or **sentence**.
It **sets the scene** for **further details**.

The **rheme** is the **rest** of the **clause** or **sentence**.
It is the **detail following** the **theme**.

Examples

- The car (theme) — is over beyond the line of trees. (rheme)
- The adults (theme) — were presenting the prizes. (rheme)

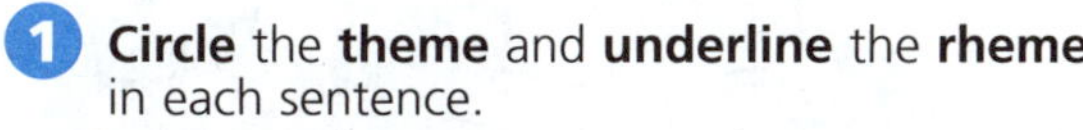

1 **Circle** the **theme** and **underline** the **rheme** in each sentence.

- **a** All of the people were at the circus.
- **b** My sister Carol has been to the village.
- **c** You and your brother have been allowed to play here.
- **d** The pony was trotting around the ring.
- **e** Joel and Jake hoped to win the race.

2 **Add** a suitable **theme** or **rheme** to **complete** these sentences.

- **a** ______________________________ were able to complete the task.
- **b** Some old earthmoving gear ______________________________.
- **c** Those valuable jewels ______________________________.
- **d** ______________________________ are in the grassy fields.
- **e** She ______________________________.

It is possible for a sentence or clause to be **written in different ways** so that in one sentence a phrase may be the **theme**, and in the other it may be the **rheme**.

Example

- **The girl** had practised the movement. (The girl is the theme.)
- The movement **had been practised by the girl**. (The girl is part of the rheme.)

3 **Write each sentence in a different form** so that the word or phrase in **bold** is the **rheme**.

- **a** **They** broke the vase yesterday morning.

____

- **b** **Verity and Rohan** were collecting the firewood.

____

4 **Write each sentence** in a **different form** so that the **word** or **phrase** in **bold** is the **theme**.

- **a** The stamps had been taken by **the boy**.

____

- **b** My uncle was polishing **the car**.

____

Answers on page 127

Word groups and phrases

Word groups and **phrases** can be built around a **main** or **head word**.

Examples

- She gave him a bright yellow **raincoat**.
  (noun group, head word *raincoat*)
- The work had not been **completed** yet.
  (verb group, head word *completed*)
- He finished the artwork so very **carefully**.
  (adverb group, head word *carefully*)
- It was an exceptionally attractive **antique** statue.
  (adjective group, head word *antique*)

1 **Underline** the **noun groups**.

a Several of them began the long exhausting march to the hills.

b Many small young kittens were in the house.

c The weather-beaten old sea-captain leaned over the railing.

d They arrived at the brightly lit new supermarket.

e The tall female athletes from nearby joined the game.

2 **Underline** the **verb groups**.

a She said he might have broken the vase.

b Mike may have been weaving the jacket.

c Mark has not been finishing the painting today.

d The adults should have been setting a good example.

e They had been seen by the visitors many times.

3 **Circle** the **adjective** or **adverb groups**. **Identify** them as adjectives or adverbs.

a There was the bright red restored vehicle. ____________________

b They travelled extremely quickly to the town. ____________________

c A large, wilting, red rose was in the vase. ____________________

d Many strange new inventions were on display. ____________________

e The car was very extensively damaged. ____________________

4 **a** **Use** *small, bright, yellow spade* as a **noun group** in a **sentence**.

____

b **Use** *might have provided* as a **verb group** in a **sentence**.

____

c **Use** *quite often* as an **adverb group** in a **sentence**.

____

d **Use** *nine new colourful* as an **adjective group** in a **sentence**.

____

5 Look at the **word groups** in **bold** and write the **type** of word group in the brackets.

There in the middle of a **dark, damp forest** (________________________) was a hut that **had not been lived** (________________________) in for **many, many long** (________________________) years.

Answers on page 127

Connectives and cohesion

Connectives join words, phrases and **clauses** to create **longer simple** or **compound sentences**. The words *and*, *but* and *or* are the **most common connectives**.

Cohesion links ideas, **words** and **sentences** to form **meaningful** sentences and paragraphs. **Connectives play** an **important role** in **cohesion**.

Examples

- They went to town **and** went shopping.
- She visited her friend **because** she was sick.
- **As** he went inside, he noticed how cold the house was.

and, *because* and *as* are **connectives**.

- She collected the parcel on Monday **or** on Tuesday.
- They agreed **that** it was difficult to solve.

The **connectives** *or* and *that* **bind** the **text** and **create cohesion**.

1 **Underline** the **connectives** in these sentences.

a They visited the zoo but did not stay long.
b When you are able you should finish this task.
c They will set out before the sun rises.
d Can you collect the books because I will be too late?
e Although he was early, he did not watch the film.

2 Write sentences **using connectives** to **join** the following **words**.

a two adverbs: ______________________________

____

b three nouns: ______________________________

____

c two adjective groups: ______________________________

____

3 **Combine** these pairs of sentences using **connectives**. **Underline** the connectives.

a They will leave at dawn. They may leave at nine o'clock.

____

b She saw the light. She did not turn it off.

____

c Eleni was in bed. She could not finish the work.

____

4 **Read** the sentences. Are the words in **bold connectives**?

a He worked on **although** he was very tired. Yes ☐ No ☐ *(tick)*
b When we get **there** we will take it away. Yes ☐ No ☐
c **Are** the birds in the shrubs but not in the trees? Yes ☐ No ☐

Answers on page 127

Section test 5B

1 **Read** the sentences and **identify** them as **indicative**, **imperative** or **subjunctive mood**.

a Collect the present from the counter. ________________

b An army of builders arrived at the scene. ________________

c He hoped that it be recovered. ________________

2 **Add** a suitable **verb of the mood shown** to these sentences.

a ________________ towards the scrub at once. (imperative)

b She wished she ________________ at home. (subjunctive)

c There ________________ very few people at the zoo. (indicative)

3 Identify the **mood of the verb** in **bold** and state whether it is an **action**, **feeling or thinking**, **telling or saying**, or **having** or **being** verb.

The explorers **are travelling** towards the distant mountain.

Mood ________________ Form of verb ________________

4 **Circle** the **theme** and **underline** the **rheme** in each sentence.

a Many of the plants grew well in the yard.

b He cannot play the game very well.

c She and her sister read the new novel.

5 **Write sentences** using these **word groups**.

a Use *large, wide, picket fence* as a **noun group**.

____

b Use *very rarely* as an **adverb group**.

____

c Use *could be blamed* as a **verb group**.

____

d Use *several small colourful* as an **adjective group**.

____

6 Look at the word groups in **bold** and **write** the **type** of **word group** in the brackets.

Very cautiously, (________________) the **tiny yellow-furred** (________________) creature emerged from its hole.

7 **Underline** the **connectives** in these sentences.

a The group went to the shop or to the centre.

b Take the books away because I do not need them.

c She was so tired that she could not concentrate.

8 Use *if he could* in a sentence so that *if* is the **connective**.

____

Answers on pages 127–128

Review test 5

1 Are the word groups in **bold participants**?

a **Some of the cattle** were in the pavilion. Yes ☐ No ☐ *(tick)*

b **Early in the week** we went on an excursion. Yes ☐ No ☐

c The car **had been hit** by hailstones. Yes ☐ No ☐

d Will **you and your sister** find the pencils? Yes ☐ No ☐

e Many of them prepared **the backdrop**. Yes ☐ No ☐

2 **Study** the sentences and **label** the **parts** as **participant**, **process**, **attribute** or **circumstance**.

a By the road ______________

a huge flock of birds ______________

had gathered ______________

to eat the scraps. ______________

b Alison and her sister Kate ______________

had been playing ______________

in a happy and contented way ______________

for several hours. ______________

c All this time ______________

several small brown ______________

birds from the north ______________

had begun to fly ______________

to their breeding grounds. ______________

3 **Replace** the **participants** and **processes** underlined with ones of your **own choice**.

a Those clever monkeys were enjoying themselves on the ropes.

____

b The boy in the red cap was entering the building quietly.

____

c Have you and Tim been able to investigate the matter?

____

4 **Circle** the **noun groups** in these sentences and **underline** any **attributes**.

a She collected the long, white, narrow, cardboard tubes.

b All the skilful, young players entered the contest.

c The short, narrow, mud-stained cloth was near the gate.

5 **Write** a **sentence** using the **circumstance** with the **form** of the **verb** listed.

a *frequently*, action verb group:

____

b *at nightfall*, having or being verb group:

____

Answers on page 128

6 **Add** a suitable **verb** of the **mood** shown to these sentences.

a ____________ to the supermarket for me. (imperative)

b I hope that I ____________ the work soon. (subjunctive)

c They all ____________ the box to the truck. (indicative)

7 **Use** the **verb** and **mood** shown to **create your own sentence**.

a *drew*, indicative:

____

b *stop*, imperative:

____

c *believe*, subjunctive:

____

8 **Add** a suitable **theme or rheme** to **complete** these sentences.

a The young girl ____________.

b ____________ sat next to the stranger.

c Several young birds ____________.

9 a **Change** the **form** of this sentence so that the part in **bold** becomes the **rheme** of a **new sentence**.

The smart operator had finished the job before time.

____

b **Change** the **form** of this sentence so that the part in **bold** becomes the **theme** of a **new sentence**.

The plan had been developed by **the whole team**.

____

10 **Identify** the parts of these sentences in **bold** as **noun**, **verb**, **adjective** or **adverb groups**.

a There is a **neat collection of sports cards**. ____________

b **Many newly hatched, featherless** birds were in the nest. ____________

c **Slowly, sadly and painfully** the explorers returned. ____________

d Charmaine **had been collecting** stamps for years. ____________

11 **Combine** these **pairs** of **sentences**. **Underline** the **connectives**.

a She will visit the town. She may visit her relatives.

____

b Did you see the book? Did you put it back?

____

c Jeremy was very tired. He did not sleep well last night.

____

d Collect the pencils. You must stay here to do it.

____

Answers on page 128

Dictionary of grammatical terms

		Page
Adjectival clause	An adjectival clause describes a noun or pronoun in one of the other clauses in a sentence. Adjectival clauses begin with a relative pronoun (*who*, *whom*, *whose*, *which*, *that*) and contain a finite verb.	64–66
Adjectival phrase	An adjectival phrase describes nouns or pronouns and therefore does the work of an adjective. These phrases usually begin with a preposition and do not contain a finite verb.	51
Adjective	An adjective is a describing word. It tells us what kind of, how many, how much or which person or object is being described.	10–13
	• Demonstrative: pointing out or identifying	11
	• Descriptive: describing or telling about	10
	• Distributive: pointing out or identifying separate things	11
	• Indefinite: no actual number	11
	• Numbering: pointing out how many	10
	• Proper: nationalities	10
Adverb	An adverb is a word that describes or modifies other words, such as verbs, adjectives or other adverbs. Many adverbs tell us how, when or where.	22–23
	• Adverbs of degree are those that indicate to what extent something is done or happens. Many of these adverbs really tell how something is done.	23
	• Interrogative adverbs are those that begin questions. They begin questions related to how, when, where or why.	22
	• Negative adverbs create negative sentences. Two common negative adverbs are *not* and *never*.	23
	• Numerical adverbs indicate how many times an action takes place: *twice* and *thrice* are two numerical adverbs.	23
Adverbial clause	Adverbial clauses do the work of an adverb. They can tell how, when, where or why an action takes place. They begin with a conjunction and contain a finite verb.	67–68
	They can also show: • the condition under which something is done • a comparison between things • a concession or the granting of something • the result of an action • the purpose for which some action was done.	
Adverbial phrase	A phrase is a group of words without a finite verb. An adverbial phrase tells us about a verb. It does the work of an adverb. Adverbial phrases usually begin with a preposition.	52
Article	Articles are a special kind of adjective. There are three articles: *a*, *an* and *the*. *A* and *an* are indefinite articles because they do not refer to a particular object. *The* is called the definite article because it refers to a specific object.	12
Attribute	An attribute is a word or phrase that adds to the meaning of a noun or pronoun. It is an adjective or adjectival phrase.	97

Dictionary of grammatical terms

		Page
Case	Case is a feature of nouns and pronouns. It is the relationship between these nouns and pronouns and other words in a sentence. • Nominative: The key word in the subject is nominative case subject of the verb. The key word in the complement is nominative case complement of the verb. • Objective: The key word in the object is objective case governed by the verb. Nouns or pronouns can also be objective case governed by a preposition, verbal noun or a participle. • Possessive: The possessive case is shown by the apostrophe. The apostrophe shows ownership.	43–46 43 44–45 46
Circumstance	Circumstances are words or phrases that tell us how, when, where or why. They are adverbs or adverbial phrases.	98
Cohesion	Cohesion links ideas, words and sentences to form meaningful sentences and paragraphs. Connectives play an important role in cohesion.	103
Command or request	A command or request is a simple sentence that requires an action or response.	57
Complement	Complements are found in sentences with being verbs. The being verb links the subject and the complement.	35
Complex sentence	A complex sentence is made up of two or more clauses. One of the clauses is the principal clause and the other clauses are called subordinate clauses. Subordinate clauses can do the work of adjectives, adverbs or nouns.	60
Compound sentence	A compound sentence is made up of two or more parts called clauses. These clauses are joined by the conjunctions *or*, *and* or *but*.	59
Compound-complex sentence	A compound-complex sentence is made up of three or more clauses. It contains two or more principal clauses and one or more subordinate clauses. The subordinate clauses can do the work of adjectives, adverbs or nouns.	61
Conjunction	A conjunction is a joining word. It links together single words, phrases and clauses. • Coordinating: The most common coordinating conjunctions are *and*, *but* and *or*. • Subordinating: Subordinating conjunctions join two or more clauses together. One is the main clause (principal clause), the others are subordinate clauses (often adverbial clauses).	25
Connective	Connectives join words, phrases and clauses to create longer sentences, either simple or compound. The words *and*, *but* and *or* are the most common connectives.	103
Exclamatory sentences	An exclamatory sentence is a simple sentence that shows strong feeling. It has an exclamation mark (!) at the end.	58
Gender	Gender is a feature of nouns and pronouns. There are four genders (masculine, feminine, common, neuter).	40

Dictionary of grammatical terms

Term	Definition	Page
Infinitive phrase	An infinitive phrase begins with an infinitive and can be used in different ways in sentences. It can act as an adverb, adjective, subject, object or complement.	54
Interjection	Interjections are usually short words that express sudden feeling. They are followed by an exclamation mark (!).	26
Interrogative sentence	An interrogative sentence is one that asks a question. A question requires a spoken or written answer.	58
Mood	Mood is a term we use to show how a process (verb) is used in a sentence. • Indicative mood expresses a fact. • Imperative mood expresses a command. • Subjunctive mood expresses hopes or wishes.	100
Noun	A noun is a naming word. It is the name of a person, animal, place, thing, feeling or idea. • Abstract nouns are the names of feelings and ideas. • Collective nouns are the names of a collection of people or things. • Common nouns are the names of common things of the same kind. • Proper nouns are the names of particular persons or places and begin with a capital letter.	1–3 2 2 1 1
Noun clause	A noun clause begins with a conjunction. It can be the subject, object or complement of a verb in another clause. It can be the object of a participle, preposition or verbal noun.	70–71
Number	Number is a feature of nouns and pronouns. If the noun or pronoun stands for one thing it is called a singular noun. If the noun or pronoun stands for more than one thing it is called a plural noun.	39
Object	• A direct object is the person or thing acted on by the subject in a sentence. • An indirect object is the person or thing who receives the direct object.	33 34
Participant	Participants are the persons, places, ideas and things that take part in the action or discussion in a sentence. In most cases participants are subjects or objects.	95
Participle phrase	A phrase is a group of words without a finite verb. A participle phrase does the work of an adjective. It begins with a past or present participle.	54
Person	Person is a feature of personal pronouns and nouns. There are three persons: first, second and third. • The actual persons speaking are called first person. • Those persons being spoken to are called second person. • Persons being spoken about are called third person.	38
Phrase	A phrase is a group of words without a finite verb.	51
Predicate	A sentence can be divided into parts—one part is called the subject, the other is called the predicate. The verb is included in the predicate.	32

Dictionary of grammatical terms

		Page
Preposition	A preposition is a word that begins a phrase. It usually has a noun or pronoun after it. Common prepositions are *to*, *at*, *in*, *of*, *by*, *up*, *across*, *past*, *with*, *from*, *over*, *around*, *after*, *among*, *between*.	26
Process	Processes are the action or state of being verbs. They can be described as action verb groups, thinking or feeling verb groups, telling or saying verb groups, or having or being verb groups.	96
Pronoun	A pronoun is a word that can be used instead of a noun.	6–8
	• Demonstrative pronouns stand instead of the name of the object. They are *this*, *that*, *these* and *those*.	8
	• Distributive pronouns are used to point out a particular item. They are *each*, *either* and *neither*.	8
	• Indefinite pronouns do not stand for any particular person, thing or place. They end in *one*, *body* or *thing*.	8
	• Interrogative pronouns are used at the beginning of a sentence.	7
	• Personal pronouns are used in place of actual names of people.	6
	• Possessive pronouns own something.	6
	• Reflexive pronouns end in *self* or *selves*. They refer to a previous noun or pronoun.	6
	• Relative pronouns begin an adjectival clause in a sentence with two or more clauses. Relative pronouns are *who*, *whom*, *whose*, *which* and *that*.	7
Rheme	The theme is the first part of a clause or sentence. It sets the scene for further details. The rheme is the rest of the clause or sentence. It is the detail following the theme.	101
Statement	A statement is a simple sentence that states a fact, opinion or possibility.	57
Subject	A sentence can be divided into parts and one part is called the subject. To find the subject you must first find the verb. The subject performs the action of the verb.	31
Tense	Verbs are written in such a way that you can tell when an action or happening is taking place. This is what is called the tense of the verb. There are three main tenses: present tense, past tense, future tense.	16
Theme	The theme is the first part of a clause or sentence. It sets the scene for further details. It is possible for a sentence or clause to be written in different ways so that in one sentence a phrase may be the theme and in another it may be the rheme.	101

Dictionary of grammatical terms

		Page
Verb	A verb tells us what is being done—it is a doing, having or being word. Verbs can be action verbs, feeling or thinking verbs, stating or telling words, or relating words.	15–18
	• Main verbs are those that stand alone but some verbs are made up of two or more verbs. Those extra verbs that are put with the main verb are called auxiliary verbs.	15
	• Where there is a main verb and one or more auxiliary verbs the complete verb is called a compound verb.	15
	• An infinite verb, called the infinitive, is never the main verb in a sentence. It almost always begins with the word *to* and frequently begins a group of words called a phrase.	18
	• Verbs are often made up of auxiliary verbs and participles (past participles and present participles). Past participles indicate past tense. Present participles indicate present tense.	17
	• Regular verbs are those in which the past participle ends in *ed*, *d* or *t*.	17
	• Irregular verbs are those in which the past tense and the past participle are formed in a different way.	17
Verbal noun phrase	A verbal noun phrase does the work of a noun. It begins with a verbal noun. It can be used in different ways in sentences. It can be used as a subject, object or complement and can be the object of a preposition.	53
Voice	Verbs can be active voice or passive voice. The two different voices allow the same thoughts or ideas to be expressed in two different ways.	18

Answers

1 Parts of speech

Page 1

1 **a** watch, table, telephone **b** parcel, shop, road

2 **a** book, desk **b** girl, towel, beach **c** father, meat, supermarket

3 **a** Jill, Jan **b** Mittens, Tim

Quick check

Common: sun, children, township, people, jetty, shape, shark, water, jetty, creature.
Proper: Wednesday, Lonton, Raynor, Sharnie, Mike, John

Page 2

1 **a** flock, herd **b** hand, bunch **c** litter, colony

2 **a** flight **b** swarm **c** team

3 **a** bravery **b** sorrow **c** beauty

4 **a** pleasure **b** relief **c** sorrow

Page 3

1 **a** growing **b** dancing **c** building

2 **a** screaming **b** climbing **c** adjusting

3 **a** verbal noun **b** part of verb **c** part of verb **d** verbal noun **e** part of verb, verbal noun

Quick check

1 **a** raising **b** completing **c** accelerating **d** dividing

2 (Sample answer) Collecting the shells took several hours.

Page 4

1 (Sample answers) **a** shiny, new **b** long, dusty

2 (Sample answers) **a** many young **b** the three

3 **a** with red buttons **b** that were of modern design **c** that has a pink door

Quick check

1 **a** a large number of beautiful paintings **b** the car with the red roof **c** many of the goods that were on the shelf **d** some of the people from out of town

2 (Sample answer) These delightful fresh flowers were placed in a vase.

Page 5 Nouns: How much do you know?

1 **a** tribe, clearing, jungle **b** cars, garages **c** pictures, wall

2 Jim, Jae, Atherton, Thursday, Ford, Lake Barrine, Leeanne, John, Eachem Road

3 **a** flight, herd **b** litter, bunches **c** groups, fleet

4 grief, death, grief, anger, kindness, love

5 **a** camping, fishing **b** collecting, mounting **c** caring

6 (Sample answers) **a** collecting **b** dividing **c** growing

7 (Sample answers) **a** children and adults **b** Lisa and Sharon **c** swimming **d** pride **e** admiration

Page 6

1 **a** he **b** you, them **c** we, it

2 (Sample answers) **a** you, I **b** we **c** they

3 **a** yours **b** our **c** your

4 (Sample answers) **a** her **b** his **c** our

5 **a** herself **b** yourselves **c** themselves

6 (Sample answers) **a** yourself **b** itself

Page 7

1 **a** that—that I own **b** who—who owns the helmet **c** whose—whose father is away

2 **a** whose **b** that/which **c** that/which

3 (Sample answers) **a** that travelled from Sydney **b** which was in the hall **c** who had entered the contest

4 **a** which **b** who **c** what

Page 8

1 **a** those **b** these **c** that

2 (Sample answers) **a** these **b** this **c** that

3 **a** neither **b** each **c** either

4 **a** anybody **b** everything **c** no-one **d** something

Answers

Page 9 Pronouns: How much do you know?

1 **Personal:** they, I, you. **Possessive:** ours. **Reflexive:** themselves, yourself

2 (Sample answers) **a** they, themselves **b** she, hers **c** we, our

3 **a** that—that I own **b** which—which has been cleaned **c** whose—whose mother is at the gate

4 **a** that, which **b** whose **c** who

5 **a** who **b** what **c** which

6 **a** these **b** that **c** those

7 **a** each **b** neither **c** either

8 **a** anybody **b** someone **c** somebody

Page 10

1 **a** fifteen **b** nine **c** third

2 (Sample answers) **a** two **b** seven **c** fourth

3 **a** bright, peaceful **b** motor, safe **c** young, beautiful

4 (Sample answers) **a** wide, exciting **b** store, terrible **c** new, green

5 **a** Spanish **b** Irish **c** South Australian

Quick check

Numbering: first, eleven. **Descriptive:** motor, calm, beautiful, delightful, local, crowded. **Proper:** African

Page 11

1 **a** those **b** this **c** this

2 **a** neither **b** either **c** every

3 (Sample answers) **a** every, each **b** every

4 **a** few **b** most **c** less

5 (Sample answers) **a** several **b** some

Quick check

(Sample answers) those, every, many, each

Page 12

1 **a** which **b** what **c** whose

2 **a** adjective **b** pronoun **c** adjective **d** pronoun

Quick check

Interrogative adjectives: what, whose. **Interrogative pronouns:** which, who. **Articles:** the, a, the, a, the

Page 13

1 **a** smaller, smallest **b** kinder, kindest **c** heavier, heaviest **d** brighter, brightest

2 **a** more/less splendid … most/least splendid **b** more/less careful … most/least careful **c** more/less fierce … most/least fierce

Page 14 Adjectives: How much do you know?

1 (Sample answers) **a** tall, young, exciting, grassy **b** small, large **c** new, fine, second

2 **a** African **b** Indonesian **c** Chinese

3 (Sample answers) **a** those **b** these **c** that **d** each **e** either

4 **a** some **b** many **c** more

5 **a** interrogative adjective **b** interrogative pronoun **c** interrogative adjective **d** interrogative pronoun

6 (Sample answers) **a** a, the **b** an, the **c** a, an, the

7 **a** larger, largest **b** taller, tallest **c** useful, most/least useful **d** bad, worse **e** much, most

Page 15

1 **a** delivered, action **b** howled, stating or telling **c** forgot, thinking or feeling **d** became, relating

2 (Sample answers) **a** remember **b** lifted **c** shouted **d** is

3 **a** <u>will</u> travel **b** <u>can</u> complete **c** <u>did</u> remove

4 (Sample answers) **a** has completed **b** will take **c** have fixed

5 **a** will have broken **b** have been collected **c** may have sprinted

Page 16

1 **a** enjoy, present **b** collected, past **c** will build, future **d** was driven, past **e** had completed, past

Answers

2 (Sample answers) **a** attend **b** planted **c** will leave **d** searched

3 **b** travelled **c** will travel **e** fixed **f** will fix

4 **a** will speed **b** collect **c** fertilised

Quick check

1 will read—future

2 had taken—past

3 will be polished—future

4 were watered—past

Page 17

1 **a** painted, past **b** flying, present **c** cried, past **d** jumping, present

2 (Sample answers) **a** found, past **b** thrown, past **c** dancing, present **d** blown, past

3 **a** rubbed, rubbed **b** stopped, stopped **c** delayed, delayed **d** cried, cried

4 **a** sprang, sprung **b** chose, chosen **c** rode, ridden **d** tore, torn

Page 18

1 **a** to finish, yes **b** to sleep, yes **c** to catch, yes **d** to succeed, no

2 (Sample answers) **a** to finish the work **b** to paint the wall **c** to collect the money **d** to reach the summit

3 **a** was groomed, passive **b** completed, active **c** were eaten, passive **d** trampled, active

Quick check

Infinitives: to play, to enjoy, to purchase, to draw. **Active voice verbs:** came, began, visited, posted

Page 19 Verbs: How much do you know?

1 **a** cooked, action **b** forgot, thinking or feeling **c** cried, stating or telling **d** were, relating

2 **a** has painted **b** will replace **c** had travelled

3 **a** followed, past **b** will sail, future **c** has decided, past **d** decorate, present

4 **a** will be driven **b** will play

5 **a** shown **b** practising **c** cleaned

6 **a** cracked, cracked, cracking **b** blew, blown, blowing **c** shrank, shrunk, shrinking

7 **a** to read **b** to exchange **c** to follow **d** to catch

8 **a** was painted, passive **b** chewed, active **c** was damaged, passive **d** were picked, passive

Pages 20–21 Section test 1A

1 **Common nouns:** children, picnic, group, afternoon, area, time, time, group, homes. **Proper nouns:** Welling Crossing, Alan, Rae, Daville, Scott Highway

2 **a** flock **b** pride **c** fleet

3 **Abstract nouns:** love, enjoyment. **Verbal nouns:** galloping, parasailing

4 (Sample answers) **a** the young children **b** your nephews and nieces

5 **Personal pronouns:** you, I. **Possessive pronouns:** your, his, theirs. **Reflexive pronouns:** yourself

6 **a** that—that were on the edge of the forest **b** which—which belongs to Erica

7 (Sample answers) **a** Who is going to the beach? **b** What is the time?

8 (Sample answers) **a** anyone **b** everybody **c** no-one

9 **a** each **b** either

10 **Numbering:** seven, five. **Descriptive:** tall, largest, blue, huge, fine. **Proper:** Swedish, Dutch, English

11 (Sample answers) **a** I saw those cars. **b** That book is mine.

12 (Sample answers) **a** every **b** each

13 **a** several **b** some **c** most

14 (Sample answers) **a** What time is it? **b** Whose watch has been lost? **c** Which car went to the game?

15 **a** smaller **b** most **c** more or less careful

16 (Sample answer) The work might be completed soon.

17 (Sample answer) They will find the basket at the edge of the forest.

18 **a** yes **b** no

19 **a** chose, chosen, choosing **b** drove, driven, driving

Answers

Page 22

1 **a** carefully, how **b** soon, when **c** there, where **d** later, when **e** inside, where

2 (Sample answers) **a** She spoke angrily to the boy. **b** They will go away soon. **c** She soon collected the pencils.

3 **a** around **b** over **c** yesterday **d** promptly **e** everywhere **f** often

4 **a** where **b** when **c** how

Page 23

1 **a** The boy has not gone into the city. **b** She has not always collected the flowers in the garden.

2 **a** extremely sick **b** unbearably hot **c** nearly impossible

3 **a** nearer, nearest **b** more/less sadly, most/least sadly **c** more/less dangerously, most/least dangerously

Page 24 Adverbs: How much do you know?

1 (Sample answers) **a** quickly **b** soon **c** there **d** immediately **e** hard

2 **a** The boys worked noisily. **b** She often went with him. **c** Do not go outside.

3 (Sample answers) **a** How are you travelling? **b** Where is the gauge? **c** When are you leaving?

4 **a** smartly **b** beautifully **c** noisily

5 **a** They did not visit the spot. **b** I do not always see him.

6 **a** quite **b** really **c** tightly **d** comfortably

7 **b** earlier **c** earliest

8 **a** harder, hardest **b** more/less clumsily, most/least clumsily

Page 25

1 **a** and, words **b** or, phrases **c** but, clauses

2 **a** but **b** or **c** and

3 **a** after **b** though **c** if

4 **a** either, or **b** both, and **c** not, but

Page 26

1 **a** of—of the students, to—to the farm, by—by the lake **b** from—from the zoos, over—over the mountains **c** past—past the yard, along—along the fence

2 (Sample answers) **a** in, by **b** near, with **c** at, in

3 **a** adverb **b** preposition **c** preposition **d** adverb

4 **a** They will leave after. **b** After the picnic they went home.

5 **a** wow **b** oh **c** ouch **d** bravo

Pages 27–28 Section test 1B

1 **a** above **b** angrily **c** slowly **d** very **e** away **f** quietly

2 (Sample answers) **a** They will leave soon. **b** It was a hugely successful fete. **c** I go there often.

3 (Sample answers) **a** where **b** when **c** why

4 **a** Harriet has not left for her music lesson. **b** Craig does not always wash the car on Sunday.

5 **a** too—quickly **b** almost—five **c** partly—finished

6 (Sample answers) **a** slowly **b** wearily **c** carefully **d** badly **e** happily

7 **b** more tightly **c** most tightly

8 (Sample answers) **a** or **b** and **c** but

9 **a** and—in the evening, at sunrise **b** or—his brother Steve, his cousin Ray **c** but—She returned the book, she had not finished reading it

10 **a** after **b** wherever **c** because

11 (Sample answer) They will go if they are allowed.

12 (Sample answer) Not one but several fish were caught.

13 **a** to—to the shop, in—in the afternoon **b** by—by night, for—for the missing dog **c** near—near the stable, beyond—beyond the water trough

14 (Sample answers) **a** in, at **b** near **c** of, by

Answers

15 **a** adverb **b** adverb **c** preposition **d** preposition **e** adverb

16 **a** eek **b** oops **c** hush

Pages 29–30 Review test 1

1 (Sample answers) **a** boys, Alongi **b** May, Jensen, city **c** team, footballers, Langton **d** pain, distress

2 **a** riding **b** collecting **c** cultivating

3 (Sample answers) **a** wagon with a heavy load **b** the beautiful roses in the vases **c** the youngest and fittest workers

4 (Sample answers) **Common:** bread, butter, bale, book. **Proper:** Brisbane, Brian, Barry, Ballarat. **Collective:** batch, brood, bouquet, bunch. **Abstract:** beauty, belief, badness, bliss

5 (Sample answers) **a** she, his **b** your, us **c** herself **d** that **e** who **f** several **g** this **h** each

6 (Sample answer) Here is the car that I own.

7 **Numbering:** nine. **Descriptive:** deep, blue, green, large. **Proper:** Russian, Mascot, American. **Demonstrative:** this

8 **a** distributive **b** indefinite

9 (Sample answer) What colour is it?

10 **b** more careful **c** most/least careful

11 (Sample answer) He <u>has been repairing</u> the vehicle.

12 The mechanic will adjust the brakes.

13 (Sample answers) **a** painted **b** cleaning **c** photographed

14 **a** to read **b** to hear

15 **a** later, when **b** cheerfully, how **c** there, where

16 **a** quite <u>ill</u> **b** terribly <u>windy</u>

17 (Sample answers) **a** John or Joan will go to the movies. **b** They will leave if they can.

18 (Sample answer) They searched above the cupboard, on the floor and at the fireplace.

19 yes—it tells where

20 (Sample answer) Ah! You have found it.

2 Sentence parts and features

Page 31

1 **a** collected—<u>Many of the boys</u> **b** are building—<u>Some friends of ours</u> **c** studied—<u>The scientist</u>

2 **a** The police officers **b** The garbage truck **c** My young sister

3 **a** will be wearing—<u>Karen</u> **b** swam—<u>The young girl</u> **c** will select—<u>Bob</u>

Page 32

1 **a** were damaged—<u>were damaged by the hail</u> **b** attended—<u>attended the meeting yesterday</u> **c** were placed—<u>were placed in the paddock</u> **d** was made—<u>was made by the boys</u> **e** was left—<u>was left in storage</u>

2 **a** a diamond ring near the gate **b** grazing in the paddock **c** in Crown Street

3 (Sample answers) **a** <u>entered</u> the contest last week **b** <u>was leaning</u> against the house **c** <u>climbed</u> the tall fence

4 **a** has been working—<u>has been working here all day</u> **b** grazed—<u>near the lake, by the homestead</u> **c** can find—<u>a glue stick, where</u> **d** rushed—<u>down from the bridge, wildly</u>

Page 33

1 **a** recognised—<u>her cousin</u> **b** collects—<u>stamps</u> **c** carried—<u>its load</u> **d** hunted—<u>the bison</u> e studied—<u>that subject</u>

2 (Sample answers) **a** was carrying—the heavy parcel **b** had eaten—the apples **c** saw—the green car

3 **a** yes—instructions **b** no **c** yes—the work **d** no

4 **a** yes—the car **b** no **c** yes—a beautiful ballad **d** yes—the ball

Page 34

1 **a** the letter, <u>his father</u> **b** the presents, <u>Nina</u> **c** the drinks, <u>Ellen</u> **d** the bucket, <u>Ken</u> **e** a brand new watch, her <u>sister</u>

2 (Sample answers) **a** the parcel to Franny **b** the book to George **c** it to him

Answers

3 **a** a new toy—Sam **b** the new costumes—the girls **c** the small package—him

4 (Sample answers) **a** me, the book **b** them, presents

Page 35

1 **a** is—his Labrador dog **b** are—Jim and Jae **c** is—a zucchini **d** am—an electrician

2 **a** a favourite with local gardeners **b** a very talented artist **c** a howling gale **d** my sister

3 **a** The African prince—proud warrior **b** our next door neighbour—a very successful writer **c** The animals on the move—migrating caribou

4 **a** The speech—long and boring **b** This room—untidy **c** The brilliant light—dull and yellow

Pages 36–37 Section test 2A

1 **a** brought—Some of the visitors **b** taught—All of the lecturers **c** was grown—This excellent crop **d** have found—I **e** is—The building with the wide staircase

2 (Sample answers) **a** The young girls **b** This student **c** All the workers

3 **a** will use—You **b** swam—the divers **c** are studying—you

4 **a** flew—over the swamp **b** remained—in the paddocks **c** was sold—last week **d** gathered—at the display centre **e** lives—in Greer Street

5 (Sample answers) **a** went to the theatre **b** built this slab hut **c** has been to England before

6 **a** have been packing—up all the year **b** travelled—by the stream across the valley **c** can see—what on the horizon

7 (Sample answer) The herd of cattle grazed in the lush fields.

8 (Sample answer) All the people recognised the spot easily.

9 **a** collected—The weary travellers—their luggage (object) **b** enjoys—His elder sister—basketball (object) **c** tidied—Some of the team—the area (object)

10 (Sample answers) **a** was taking—the girl (subject)—some of the books (object) **b** admired—All the children (subject)—the famous athletes (object) **c** glued—The student (subject)—the art work (object)

11 **a** no **b** yes—tractor parts **c** yes—a delightful poem **d** no

12 (Sample answer) He collected a box of supplies.

13 **a** the package—Kristy **b** the weapon—Sergeant Ellis **c** the broom—her **d** a fine new painting—her **e** it—me

14 **a** a new manuscript—me **b** the experiment—the people **c** a new tie—him

15 (Sample answers) **a** them—new books **b** him—a birthday present

16 **a** is—that portrait **b** are—Steve and Liam **c** is—a research scientist **d** became—the thoroughbred's companion **e** were—fine roses

17 (Sample answers) **a** old friends of ours **b** a skilful navigator **c** a famous celebrity

Page 38

1 **a** we **b** I, you **c** ours, you

2 (Sample answers) **a** I, you **b** we, yours **c** you, me

3 **a** third **b** second **c** first

4 **a** third, third, third **b** second, third, third **c** second, second, third

Page 39

1 **a** S, S, P, S, S **b** S, P, S, S **c** P, P, P, P, S

2 (Sample answers) **a** boy, pool, swim **b** girls, team, parents **c** Lauren, Marc, Philip, parks, day

3 **a** are **b** is **c** was seen **d** were

Page 40

1 **a** his (m), grandmother (f), hostess (f) **b** lad (m), his (m), niece (f), his (m), uncle's (m) **c** wife (f), hero (m)

2 **a** boat (n), children (c) **b** cattle (c), sheep (c), truck (n) **c** friend (c), holidays (n), classmates (c)

Answers

3 baron—baroness, boar—sow, bridegroom—bride, brother—sister, bull—cow, drake—duck, fox—vixen, gander—goose, duke—duchess, colt—filly

4 (Sample answers) **a** her, his **b** his, him, him **c** her, she

5 **a** his—her **b** his—her **c** his—her

Pages 41–42 Section test 2B

1 **a** I, you, me **b** we, your **c** yours, ours

2 **a** your, bag, table **b** cousin, Alan, bike, yours **c** cage, workers

3 **a** second, second **b** first, first

4 **a** She is going away. **b** Was he there? **c** My cousin and I are going.

5 **a** P, P, S, P, S **b** P, P, P, S, S **c** P, S, P, S

6 (Sample answers) **a** They drove his vehicles away. **b** Collect your parcel today.

7 (Sample answers) **a** box, rooms, corridor **b** children, papers, newsagent, shops

8 **a** were playing **b** was employed **c** were

9 **a** Joan (f), him (m), him (m) **b** Paolo (m), his (m), Gretel (f) **c** mother (f), his (m), she (f), herself (f)

10 **a** mayoress, manageress, husbands **b** uncle, nephew **c** bridesmaid, bride **d** woman's daughter, steer, ram

11 **a** mistress **b** lass **c** ewe **d** priestess **e** widow **f** princess

12 (Sample answer) We saw the lion in the park.

Page 43

1 **a** lived—man **b** have played—children **c** helped—friends

2 (Sample answers) **a** car **b** vase **c** cloud

3 **a** galloped—stallion **b** was—rat **c** is—building

4 **a** am, friend **b** are, workers **c** is, path

5 (Sample answer) That is a good question.

Page 44

1 **a** found—coin **b** failed—test **c** has collected—paintings

2 (Sample answers) **a** the swan **b** marbles **c** toys

3 **a** has delivered—letters **b** collects—stamps **c** developed—problems

4 **a** in—shade **b** at—fence **c** to—house

5 (Sample answers)
a to the dam **b** of the people **c** in the fields

Quick check

1 pegs—mailbox

2 produce—noon, farmers

Page 45

1 **a** to sell—car **b** to eat—fruit **c** to play—melody

2 (Sample answers) **a** marbles **b** the nets **c** the work

3 **a** playing—piano **b** chasing—ponies **c** planting—trees

4 (Sample answers) **a** garden **b** cards

5 **a** collecting—mail **b** eating—fruit **c** painting—fence

Page 46

1 **a** girls' clothes **b** children's books **c** Rosie's shoes **d** Mr Wong's cousins **e** Heath's friends

2 (Sample answers) **a** Amy's coat **b** Paul's car **c** Mariel's book

3 **a** Rowena's work **b** children's work **c** babies' rattles **d** women's scarves **e** boy's stamp album

4 (Sample answers) **a** bridles **b** coat

Pages 47–48 Section test 2C

1 **a** took, boy **b** visited, Ashley, Carrie, Catie **c** have been, you **d** will break, swimmer **e** raced, animals

2 (Sample answers) **a** creatures **b** Franca **c** student

3 (Sample answers) **a** pilots **b** friend **c** ones **d** students **e** dentist

4 **a** no **b** yes—job **c** no **d** yes—it **e** yes—artwork

5 **a** yes, mist, birds, into, of **b** no, stables, into **c** yes, right, left, to, to **d** yes, Melbourne, morning, from, in **e** no, August, in

6 a yes—fruit b yes—peaks c yes—bike

7 (Sample answers) a the fence (infinitive) b jeans (participle) c netball (verbal noun)

8 a horses' bridles b Neil's album c officer's rifle d girls' dresses e Nan's figurines

9 (Sample answers) a John's books b Jack's papers c Amy's clothes

10 a T, T, F b T, T, F c F, T, T

Pages 49–50 Review test 2

1 a delivered—some of the children b worked—all the scientists c had completed—Julia d are running—these wild animals e was left—the car with a red roof

2 (Sample answers) a Some of the children took b The young student collected c They did not see

3 a My eldest sister has travelled to New Zealand b You will be using which vehicle c The escapee fled quickly across the rocks d The animals wandered by the stream and along the hills

4 a cleaned, rifles b studied, work c did sing, song d was carrying, firewood e tile, floor

5 a toy, Brad b product, them c ten dollar note, him

6 a eggplant, vegetable b gymnast, Fleur c spectacular, view

7 (Sample answers) a The boy is here. b She saw the boy. c The singer is a young boy.

8 a we, you, us b I, your c ours, you

9 **Singular:** Saturday, day, it, oval, school, Torres, Cook, lunch, lunch. **Plural:** we, they, houses, sprints, jumps, relays

10 a are finishing b was found

11 a duke, sister b brother, ducks c husband, woman, stallion

12 a cattle, sheep, truck b children, park c road, horses

13 (Sample answer) The toys were given to me.

14 a jockey, railing, shed b vehicle, worker's, accident

15 (Sample answers) a The boy stealing the items will soon be discovered. b Surfing the giant waves is my passion.

3 Phrases, sentences and clauses

Page 51

1 a of damaged timber, load b with the green hat, sister c of little value, coin d with a blue cover, book e by the fence, tree

2 a with an injured leg b with the damaged sails c near the steps d with a red roof e in the bag

3 beautiful—of great beauty, mischievous—full of mischief, westerly—from the west, deep—of great depth, blue-eyed—with blue eyes

4 a from the school b through the jungle

Page 52

1 a into the village, went b by seven o'clock, were c for no reason, left d on the train, was left e after the meeting, will collect

2 (Sample answers) a in the long grass b to the celebrations c after the meeting d for their protection e at once

3 a for some time, when b in that place, where c because of problems, why d in a steady manner, how e across the pond, where

Quick check

during the day, played; in the paddock, played; because of the windy conditions, flew; above the treeline, flew; from several kilometres away, could be seen; at dusk, left

Page 53

1 a buying the car b extending the boundary fence c running the marathon d practising the piano e fixing the machine

2 (Sample answers) a Jumping the hurdles was quite easy. b They enjoyed catching butterflies.

3 a building the model—object b selecting the prizes—subject c riding in the parade—complement d wandering the highway—subject

4 (Sample answer) His favourite pastime was watching television.

Answers

5 **a** riding his trail bike **b** creating interesting artwork **c** completing crossword puzzles

Quick check

1 lifting the parcel (lifting)

2 joining the army (joining)

3 singing popular songs (singing)

Page 54

1 **a** injured in the accident (injured) **b** running towards us (running) **c** carried by the student (carried)

2 **a** found in the shipwreck **b** damaged in the fire **c** broken away

3 **a** to celebrate her birthday **b** to compete in the game

4 **a** to view the statue (subject) **b** to view the statue (object) **c** to view the statue (complement)

Pages 55–56 Section test 3A

1 **a** of many colours—coat **b** in the red shirt—brother **c** with the valuable emeralds—bracelet **d** with a green cover—book

2 **a** with the blue sails **b** with a yellow garage door **c** of blue crystal

3 **a** from the south **b** with the blue eyes

4 **a** during the morning, to the Spring Fair—went **b** by five o' clock—had completed **c** beside the road—was left **d** after the display—can leave

5 **a** at the far gate **b** during the long evening **c** on account of illness

6 **a** in comfort **b** with great care

7 with the red roof, in poor condition, near the house

8 **a** studying the subject **b** riding trail bikes **c** completing her artwork **d** mending the torn jacket

9 **a** running a marathon—subject **b** playing netball—object of preposition **c** singing on stage—complement **d** practising the piano—object

10 (Sample answers) **a** Collecting shells is interesting. **b** They had difficulty lifting the heavy weight.

11 **a** blown by the strong wind—blown **b** walking quickly—walking **c** completed correctly—completed

12 (Sample answers) **a** The car gleaming brightly was in the shed. **b** The floor washed carefully shone brightly.

13 **a** to plant the seed **b** to complete the assignment **c** to repair the engine

14 **a** adverb **b** subject **c** object **d** adjective **e** complement

15 (Sample answer) She went into the room to make the bed.

Page 57

1 **a** fact **b** opinion **c** possibility **d** fact

2 **a** Many of them changed the markings. **b** Anita and Kevin watered the garden this morning. **c** These books belong to Jonathon.

3 **a** yes, follow **b** no **c** yes, clean **d** yes, finish

Page 58

1 **a** can deliver, the children **b** are, you **c** can jump, the horse **d** did find, Hank **e** are, these apples

2 **a** I may complete the map next week. **b** She has begun that part of the artwork. **c** Peter and Michael will look after the animal.

3 **a** no **b** yes, it was/is **c** yes, she/he had

Page 59

1 **a** The man took the car and collected the parcels—and **b** He went to the beach but he did not have a swim—but **c** She will go to the show or she will stay at home—or

2 **a** The children will leave for the beach and they will take their swimming gear with them. **b** Many of them stayed at the zoo but they did not find the lost purse. **c** The young animal will cross the river or it may remain in this spot.

3 **a** and—went, played **b** but—collected, did spend **c** and—will be travelling, will be staying **d** or—will open, leave

4 **a** true, true, false (did have) **b** true, false, false

Answers

Page 60

1 **a** There is the building, that **b** She was the only person, who **c** They will leave before us, if **d** The gang toiled, that

2 **a** was brand new **b** the game will be completed **c** was held last week **d** either of her sisters

3 **a** Here are the books **b** She attended the concert **c** They played out in the yard

4 true, true, true

5 (Sample answer) There is the boy who broke the vase when he was cleaning the room.

Page 61

1 **a** No. After the party was over (S), all the relatives boarded the train (P), which was to leave at eight o' clock (S) **b** Yes. If you see the vehicle (S), which has a red roof (S), please advise the police department (P), and officers will follow it (P) **c** Yes. We will complete the task (P), and move on to the next one (P), when we are advised (S), that it is time to do so (S)

2 **a** it is a long way **b** He will go to the museum

3 was held in the concert hall, they enjoyed it very much.

4 P, S, P, S

Pages 62–63 Section test 3B

1 **a** statement **b** command **c** statement **d** interrogative **e** statement **f** exclamatory **g** interrogative **h** command

2 **a** Michelle has been to the markets. **b** The boys are sailing across the bay now. **c** The printer can have the work ready by one o'clock.

3 (Sample answers) **a** Where are you going? **b** How cold it is! **c** Hold on to it. **d** The animal crossed the road safely.

4 **a** Many of the ships were anchored in the channel. **b** (You understood) stop it here please. **c** (You understood) start the car immediately. **d** Those relatives visited him early yesterday.

5 **a** false, true, true **b** true, true, true

6 **a** or **b** or **c** and

7 All of the people collected the money and none of it was misplaced.

8 yes, yes, no (did leave)

9 **a** that—that had been used last week **b** which—which has travelled to town **c** than—than her brother is

10 **a** yes **b** The boy visited the library **c** which, so that

11 **a** we will go by train, if the bus is late, which leaves at three o'clock tomorrow **b** yes, yes, yes, when, that, and

Page 64

1 **a** that I own—that **b** which ran away—which **c** whom you knew—whom **d** whose father is sick—whose

2 **a** John saw the girls who completed the work. **b** Here are the animals that I saw. **c** This is the fence that he took away.

3 **a** She found the road. It led to the old hut. **b** The box is here. It belongs to John. **c** The woman is very ill. Her husband is away.

4 **a** broke his leg in the accident **b** was caught in the jungle trap **c** was on the lake

Quick check

1 which had a green roof

2 whose father is overseas

Page 65

1 **a** which belonged to Jessica (which, case) **b** which the Ellis family owns (that, station) **c** who scored the winning goal (who, Sam) **d** who met him at the dock (who, child)

2 **a** The boy was a stranger (whom, boy) **b** The strange weapon will be handed in (that, weapon) **c** The competition was very interesting (which, competition)

3 **a** The car that was found near the station is here. (that, car) **b** Our friend who is new to the district came here from the country. (who, friend) **c** I have a small cardboard box in which all my letters are kept. (which, box)

4 (Sample answers) **a** The boy who sat here is my brother. **b** The case that had been damaged is now repaired.

Answers

Page 66

1 **a** Many of the children ✓ we saw were very happy (whom) **b** Are these the pencils ✓ you want (that) **c** Stephanie bought the car ✓ Max sold (which) **d** In the box ✓ he put in the car were some old clothes (that)

2 (Sample answers) **a** She made the biscuits I like. (that) **b** Malcolm collected the box she had lost. (which)

3 **a** There is the new car I drove away. **b** Maria found the purse you lost at the show.

4 **a** which the tyres were thrown (into) **b** whom I spoke (of) **c** which the visitors sat (on)

5 The road along which we walked went past the farm. (along)

Page 67

1 **a** as he was told, as **b** before the sun appeared, before **c** as I was leaving the park, as **d** where the grass is green, where **e** for we could see a storm on the horizon, for

2 (Sample answers) **a** as if they were tired (how) **b** until it was dark (when) **c** where the rivers run deep (where) **d** because they had no equipment (why)

3 (Sample answers) **a** Whenever the wind blew strongly they stayed inside. **b** Lest we should lose the way we asked one of the locals.

4 **a** before I depart **b** when the sun set

Page 68

1 **a** unless the wind changes, unless **b** than her aunt is, than **c** although it was expensive, although **d** so that it might escape, so that **e** although she tried hard, although

2 (Sample answers) **a** they were sick **b** that one is **c** they complete the work **d** they could see the tigers

3 (Sample answers) **a** He hurried along so that he might escape. **b** Although the mine was abandoned they decided to visit it.

4 (Sample answers) **a** though he was feeling sick **b** if it is possible

Page 69 Adjectival and adverbial clauses: How much do you know?

1 **a** which Sam bought, which **b** whom you met, whom **c** that was left on the step, that

2 I saw the painting which Fiona had completed.

3 **a** that leads to the well (that, path) **b** who had come first (who, Ellen) **c** who came from Gosford (who, friends)

4 **a** There is the new boat Rosetta bought. (which) **b** Hugo had collected the prize he thoroughly deserved. (that)

5 **a** true, true, false, true **b** true, true, true, false

6 (Sample answers) **a** though he was sick **b** than the ones over there are

7 They collected the tools so that they could finish the work.

Page 70

1 **a** what he has done, what **b** that the cat was in the house, that **c** that the paper had been lost, that **d** when the house will be painted, when

2 **a** that we had taken the wrong turn (S) **b** that the car was brand new (O) **c** whether the gold will be found (S) **d** that it was a new book (O) **e** that they storm the barricades (C)

3 (Sample answers) **a** what he believed **b** that he had broken the lock **c** that the work is too easy

4 **a** ✓ it was not safe **b** ✓ you will succeed **c** ✓ he would be able to join them

Page 71

1 **a** what he had been told, what **b** where the kitten had hidden, where **c** what had happened, what

2 **a** where the diamonds were (verbal noun) **b** what they had seen (preposition) **c** that there was danger (participle) **d** what had been done (preposition)

3 (Sample answers) **a** Angered by what had been left behind he returned quickly. **b** She was keen on finding what had been left behind.

Answers

4 **a** that he had won the race (fact) **b** that he had been to the village (rumour) **c** that spread around the town (tidings)

Page 72 Noun clauses: How much do you know?

1 **a** what he said to me ✓ **b** after she had completed the work **c** that it had been left outside ✓ **d** that the cat was in the box ✓ **e** that had been injured

2 **a** that the car was not damaged at all (S) **b** why the boy ran home (O) **c** that she should bring the parcels (C)

3 **a** ✓ it was a great event **b** ✓ she would succeed **c** ✓ it was a dangerous climb

4 **a** That it had been damaged was unknown to them. **b** He did not know that it had been damaged.

5 **a** how it worked (verbal noun) **b** that it was urgent (participle) **c** what she had seen (preposition)

6 **a** yes, yes, no (began) **b** yes, yes

Pages 73–74 Section test 3C

1 **a** that was treated by the vet, that **b** whom I met, whom **c** whose father is interstate, whose **d** which has broken down, which **e** who lives in Adelaide, who

2 **a** The child saw the toys that were on the shelf. **b** The boy who was on the corner was quite young.

3 **a** which (saddle) **b** who (uncle) **c** that (caravan)

4 **a** This is the man who lived in the flat. **b** The house which is near here has been abandoned.

5 **a** Some of the adults ✓ we saw were very sad. **b** Are these the goods ✓ you ordered. **c** In the shed ✓ he built he stored the supplies.

6 There is the boat I bought yesterday.

7 **a** which many articles had been thrown, into **b** whom I spoke, of **c** which the robes were placed, in

8 (Sample answer) The book in which she wrote was beautifully covered.

9 **a** as if he was very tired (how) **b** when the visitors left (when) **c** where the signs had been set up (where) **d** because she needed to start straightaway (why) **e** for there was a severe hailstorm (why)

10 (Sample answers) **a** because it is too late (why) **b** when the storm was over (when)

11 **a** than her sister is, than **b** so that he could release himself, so that **c** though he was weary, though

12 (Sample answers) **a** Although it is difficult we will complete it. **b** If he sees the rubbish he will be annoyed.

13 **a** what he had really learned (O) **b** what he had really learned (S) **c** what he had really learned (C)

14 (Sample answers) **a** why it had been done **b** that it was a mistake **c** that supervision was essential

15 yes, no, yes

Pages 75–76 Review test 3

1 **a** of attractive toys (crate) **b** without a cover (book) **c** in full bloom (flowers)

2 (Sample answers) **a** with the injured leg **b** of many colours **c** on this tree

3 **a** on the new court (played) **b** by the fence (was left) **c** in the evening (take)

4 (Sample answers) **a** in the corner **b** at the corner **c** in this way

5 **a** The saddle at the stable is mine. **b** It was left at the stable.

6 **a** yes **b** yes

7 (Sample answers) **a** playing tennis **b** carving statues

8 **a** To clean the bath was an easy task. **b** The mast broken in half fell into the ocean.

9 **a** fact **b** possibility **c** opinion

10 **a** command **b** exclamatory **c** command

11 (Sample answer) What is the time?

12 Some of the people went there but none ever returned.

13 **a** principal, adjectival, adverbial **b** adverbial, adjectival, principal **c** noun, principal, adverbial, adverbial

14 Yes. It has two principal clauses and one subordinate clause.

15 (Sample answer) Although he was careful he made an error before the work was completed.

16 (Sample answers) **a** where he is going **b** that the treasure was missing

4 Syntax and correct usage

Page 77

1 ✗ Michael has spoken to him.

2 ✗ They were collecting the fruit.

3 ✓

4 ✓

5 ✗ Her sister Adele was by the creek.

6 ✗ My cousin is sailing on the lake.

Page 78

1 ✗ The group of islands is seen from the hill.

2 ✓

3 ✓

4 ✗ The list of names was on the table.

5 ✓

6 ✗ The litter of pigs was in the pen.

Page 79

1 ✗ Mike and Eloise have visited the show.

2 ✓

3 ✓

4 ✗ Laura, Paula and Claire were seen at the shop.

5 ✓

6 ✗ Several girls and boys have played the game.

Page 80

1 ✓

2 ✓

3 ✓

4 James as well as his father has been there.

5 ✓

6 ✓

Page 81

1 ✗ Neither of the cars was damaged.

2 ✓

3 ✗ Either of the boys was absent.

4 ✗ Anybody was able to finish it.

5 ✓

6 ✗ Each has won a good prize.

Page 82 Section test 4A

1 **a** 5 **b** 3 **c** 2 **d** 1 **e** 4

2 **a** Neither of the athletes has entered the event. **b** Jo and Lisa have brought in the parcel. **c** The flock of sheep is in the paddock. **d** Milton has yet to finish the work. **e** A car as well as a van is in the yard.

3 **a** has **b** are **c** has **d** was **e** has

4 **a** ✗ was—were **b** ✗ were—was **c** ✓ **d** ✗ have—has **e** ✗ are—is

5 (Sample answers) **a** has completed **b** have sold **c** has lost **d** has gone **e** was lying

Page 83

1 ✓

2 ✗ faster—fastest

3 ✗ prettiest—prettier

4 ✓

5 ✗ bigger—biggest

6 ✗ larger—largest

Page 84

1 ✗ most—more

2 ✓

3 ✓

4 ✗ more—most

5 ✓

6 ✗ more—most

Page 85

1 ✗ I live near you in the street which leads to Warra.

2 ✓

Answers

3 ✗ She crept to the room along the stairs that had a damaged railing.

4 ✗ Did you see the adult who collected the mail?

Page 86

1 ✗ rode—ridden

2 ✗ drove—driven

3 ✓

4 ✗ blew—blown

5 ✗ hid—hidden

6 ✗ sang—sung

Page 87

1 ✗ Following at a safe distance, we were confused by the fog.

2 ✗ Blown by the wind, we found the going difficult.

3 ✗ Having visited the cave, we took three hours for the journey.

4 ✓

Page 88 Section test 4B

1 a 7 b 9 c 6 d 10 e 8

2 a This is the most pleasant colour of the four you selected. b All of them have come here before. c Here is the sharpest pencil of the six on the desk. d Walking along the path we saw that the wildflowers looked pretty. e Mary saw the girl who had been in the street.

3 a longest b who c broken d most beautiful e shrunk

4 a ✓ b ✗ who—which or that c ✗ stranger—strangest d ✓ e ✗ rang—rung

5 (Sample answers) a dearest b more attractive c who d eaten e they

Page 89

1 a arose b arisen c arising

2 a begun b began c begin

3 a blew b blown c blowing

4 a break b broken c breaking

5 a choose b chosen c choose

6 a done b do c doing

7 a drew b drawn c drew

8 a known b knew

Page 90

1 a drank b drunk c drink

2 a driven b drove c driving

3 a fallen b fell c fall

4 a flown b flying

5 a given b gave c giving

6 a hidden b hid

7–9 a laid b lying c lain d lied e laid f lied g lay h lain

Page 91

1 a ridden b rode c riding

2 a rang b rung c rung

3 a rose b risen c rose

4 a seeing b seen c seeing

5 a showing b showed c shown

6 a shrank b shrunk c shrinking

7 a sang b sung c singing

8 a sank b sunk c sinking

Page 92

1 a spoken b speak c spoke

2 a sprung b sprang c springing

3 a steal b stolen c stole

4 a swim b swum c swam

5 a taken b took c take

6 a torn b tore c tear

7 a thrown b throw c thrown

8 a writing b written c wrote

Pages 93–94 Review test 4

1 a was—were b have—has c have—has d has—have e were—was f were—was g were—was h have—has i were—was

Answers

2 **a** faster—fastest **b** neatest—neater **c** beautifulest—beautiful **d** most—more **e** more—most **f** that—who **g** came—come **h** hid—hidden **i** They live near you in a town which is close to the foothills. **j** Running into the distance we noticed it became darker and darker.

3 **a** arose **b** blown **c** chosen **d** draw **e** begun **f** driven **g** flown **h** gave **i** known **j** lied **k** lying **l** ridden **m** risen **n** showed **o** shrink **p** sung **q** spoken **r** swam **s** torn **t** throw **u** written

4 **a** lain **b** lay **c** lay **d** lie

5 Functional grammar terms and usage

Page 95

1 **a** many of the sailors **b** it, thousands of repetitions **c** my young sister Meg, some of the plants **d** you and your father, the Jenolan Caves **e** the damaged old building **f** some green marbles

2 (Sample answers) **a** the young monkey **b** many of the girls **c** the old man, the parcels **d** some boys and girls, different games

3 (Sample answers) **b** A large house and a small shed were built over there. **c** He and I will go to the show.

Quick check

1 no

2 yes

3 yes

4 no

Page 96

1 **a** had been eating **b** did understand **c** had spoken **d** has been **e** will be collecting

2 **a** has practised—action **b** did understand—thinking or feeling **c** could identify—telling or saying **d** are—having or being

3 (Sample answers) **a** began **b** chopped **c** thought **d** could tell **e** were

Page 97

1 **a** many outdated (machines) **b** burning (sun), the brightly coloured (boats) **c** by the creek (oval) **d** twenty brand-new (felt pens) **e** New South Wales (team) **f** from South America (fish)

2 **a** we, <u>narrow</u>, <u>to the school hall</u> **b** <u>dense</u>, <u>small</u> boy **c** <u>those juicy</u> oranges **d** <u>happy</u> memories of <u>joyous</u> days, old **e** the woman, the pan, <u>hot</u> **f** a framework of steel

3 **a** loud, <u>was heard</u> **b** young, sick from the pain, <u>went</u> **c** marching, <u>sounded</u> **d** <u>have seen</u> **e** numerous glittering, <u>were selected</u>

4 **a** the <u>long winding</u> tracks and trails **b** The boys and girls <u>with exceptional talent</u> **c** the competitions and tournaments

Quick check (Sample answers)

1 frisky, young

2 huge, realistic

3 old dead, with long branches

Page 98

1 **a** <u>there</u>, <u>in the distance</u>—was **b** <u>at dusk</u>, <u>towards the lake</u>—moved **c** <u>across the burning sands</u>, <u>slowly</u>—moved **d** <u>with great speed</u>, <u>into space</u>—blasted **e** <u>carefully</u>—prepared

2 **a** many of the young children, <u>in the yard</u> **b** he, the small block of metal, <u>slowly and carefully</u> **c** she, <u>lately</u>, <u>to the fair</u> **d** Bryn and Janie, tennis, <u>frequently on that court</u> **e** the young filly, <u>for no reason</u>, <u>out of the yard</u>

3 (Sample answers) **a** They <u>found</u> the goods in the showground later. **b** Sometimes at dawn they <u>visit</u> the stables. **c** Towards evening they <u>sit</u> by the shed.

4 (Sample answers)

a He has seldom completed his work well. **b** They had immediately decided to visit the house. **c** She had retold the whole story by daylight. **d** They have been there before in reasonable time.

Answers

Page 99 Section test 5A

1 **a** some of the animals **b** the machine, hundreds of metal frames **c** Charles, the craft work **d** my cousin Emma **e** many small bolts

2 (Sample answers) **a** The old sea captain had been in the navy. **b** Please take a bottle of water.

3 **a** has been cleaning **b** did leave **c** were displaying **d** might have been walking

4 **a** has polished (action) **b** were listening (thinking or feeling) **c** could repeat (telling or saying)

5 **a** steamy, dense—jungle **b** many, tall, young—athletes **c** some, strong, experienced—lifters

6 (Sample answer) A rare, beautiful, handmade figurine was on the table.

7 **a** quietly, in the yard—played **b** there, in the middle of the park—rested **c** seldom—has been able **d** into the dust, beyond the mountains—journeyed

Page 100

1 **a** imperative **b** indicative **c** subjunctive **d** imperative **e** indicative

2 (Sample answers) **a** be **b** are **c** were **d** take **e** go

3 (Sample answers) **a** He raced the horse across the paddock. **b** Leave it alone. **c** I doubt we ever do it.

4 **a** indicative, action **b** imperative, action **c** subjunctive, action

Page 101

1 **a** All of the people were at the circus. **b** My sister Carol has been to the village. **c** You and your brother have been allowed to play here. **d** The pony was trotting around the ring. **e** Joel and Jake hoped to win the race.

2 (Sample answers) **a** many of the artists **b** was in the shed **c** were bought last week **d** the herds of cattle **e** had taken the book away

3 **a** The vase was broken by them yesterday morning. **b** The firewood was being collected by Verity and Rohan.

4 **a** The boy had taken the stamps. **b** The car was being polished by my uncle.

Page 102

1 **a** several of them, the long exhausting march **b** many small young kittens **c** the weather-beaten old sea-captain **d** the brightly lit new supermarket **e** the tall female athletes

2 **a** might have broken **b** may have been weaving **c** has been finishing **d** should have been setting **e** had been seen

3 **a** bright red restored—adjective **b** extremely quickly—adverb **c** large, wilting, red—adjective **d** many strange new—adjective **e** very extensively—adverb

4 (Sample answers) **a** He used a small, bright, yellow spade. **b** She might have provided the food. **c** They went there quite often. **d** Nine new colourful pieces of art were on the walls.

5 noun, verb, adjective

Page 103

1 **a** but **b** when **c** before **d** because **e** although

2 (Sample answers) **a** They walked slowly and carefully past the shed. **b** Jack and his sister Meg visited us. **c** Small brightly coloured and very noisy lorikeets could be seen.

3 **a** They will leave at dawn or at nine o'clock. **b** She saw the light but she did not turn it off. **c** Eleni could not finish the work because she was in bed.

4 **a** yes **b** no **c** no

Page 104 Section test 5B

1 **a** imperative **b** indicative **c** subjunctive

2 (Sample answers) **a** go **b** were **c** were

3 indicative, action

4 **a** Many of the plants grew well in the yard. **b** He cannot play the game very well. **c** She and her sister read the new novel.

5 (Sample answers) **a** <u>The large, wide, picket fence</u> had been built. **b** He visited us <u>very rarely</u>. **c** All of them <u>could be blamed</u>. **d** <u>Several small colourful plants</u> were in the garden.

6 adverb, adjective

7 **a** or **b** because **c** that

8 (Sample answers) He would like to go <u>if he could</u>.

Pages 105–106 Review test 5

1 **a** yes **b** no **c** no **d** yes **e** yes

2 **a** circumstance, participant, process, circumstance **b** participant, process, circumstance, circumstance **c** circumstance, attribute, participant, process, circumstance

3 (Sample answers) **a** small children—were entertaining **b** with a red shirt—was searching **c** will Jim be

4 **a** <u>long, white, narrow cardboard</u> tubes **b** All the <u>skilful young</u> players **c** <u>short narrow mud-stained</u> cloth

5 (Sample answers) **a** She <u>frequently visits</u> the old lady. **b** They <u>had been</u> there <u>at nightfall</u>.

6 **a** go **b** finish **c** loaded

7 (Sample answers) **a** He <u>drew</u> the picture on the wall. **b** <u>Stop</u> that at once. **c** I could not <u>believe</u> that he had done it.

8 (Sample answers) **a** collected the parcels **b** All the team **c** were flying into the garage

9 **a** The job was finished by the smart operator before time. **b** The whole team had developed the plan.

10 **a** noun **b** adjective **c** adverb **d** verb

11 **a** She will visit the town <u>or</u> she may visit her relatives. **b** Did you see the book <u>and</u> did you put it back? **c** Jeremy was very tired <u>because</u> he did not sleep well last night. **d** Collect the pencils <u>but</u> you must stay here to do it.